PRODUCTIVITY POWER

PRODUCTIVITY POWER

*250 Great
Ideas for
Being More
Productive*

by Jim Temme

SkillPath® Publications
Mission, KS

Editor: Kelly Scanlon

Page Layout: Mark Nothnagel

Cover Design: Rod Hankins

Illustrations: Dianne Flynn

ISBN: 978-1-878542-31-1

Library of Congress Catalog Card Number: 95-71714

37   14

Printed in the United States of America

CONTENTS

PREFACE

This book on productivity will excite you about the possibilities and potential your life offers and motivate you to action. We all have hopes and dreams. Some people manage to achieve their hopes and dreams and live up to their potential. They are productive at work and at home. They are powerful in their accomplishments.

But there are other people who just keep wishing and hoping and dreaming. They are powerless and never quite seem to accomplish anything very meaningful for themselves or others.

Productivity Power will show you how to be action-oriented. It will show you how to turn powerless statements such as "I hope to go back to school someday," into powerful, action-oriented statements like "I am returning to school in September (year) to complete my bachelor of science degree in business administration by June (year)."

Next, the book will help you develop a step-by-step action plan for turning your powerful statements into reality.

Finally, *Productivity Power* will show you how to deal with the obstacles that keep you from accomplishing your important goals, objectives, and activities—such things as daily people interruptions, phone calls, too much paperwork, stacks of mail, and unproductive meetings.

As you read each of the 250 ideas in this book, undoubtedly, you will occasionally come across a concept or idea and say to yourself, "Hey, I know that!" Believe me, you already know more than you think you do. As Somerset Maugham said, "Basic truths are too important to be new." Unfortunately, sometimes we suppress what we already know. We can become so busy just trying to get through the day that we might not consider the most efficient, effective, and productive means for accomplishing our work and personal tasks. In other words, our approach to life is often reactive rather than proactive.

This book will help you to "dust off your tool box" so that you can use many of the tools you already are aware of. Being aware of the tools at your disposal can give you more options for dealing with life events. And having more choices gives you more freedom in making decisions, which puts you in control of your own life and, ultimately, gives you more power.

So, in part, *Productivity Power* is designed to reacquaint you with what you already know but perhaps haven't been using. You already know, for instance, that procrastination is a productivity killer. But just knowing it won't necessarily cause you to change. To achieve productivity power, you must know what to do about procrastination and then take action.

> *"Whatever you do or think, you begin it. Boldness has genius, power and magic in it."*
>
> Goethe

I suggest reading the chapters of *Productivity Power* in order, but it's OK to start with any chapter. If, for example, you feel that you immediately need to learn more about how to work effectively with your supervisor for greater productivity, then by all means start with that section.

This book is the culmination of my years of study and experience, both as an employee and as a manager. Many of the ideas in the book are confirmed as powerful techniques for productivity based on informal interviews with people I've done consulting work for and who have attended my seminar presentations.

Enjoy reading *Productivity Power* and use it for years to come as a way to get more out of life. Become powerful!

Jim Temme

ACKNOWLEDGMENTS

Preparing this book was indeed a labor of love. Writing, like many things in life, requires diligence, patience, and discipline—characteristics that don't come easily to any of us. There were, however, people and experiences that helped put me back on course to finish this book when I started to stray.

First, as a public speaker, I wish to acknowledge my audiences—the broad array of interesting and interested people I have communicated with throughout the years. They have helped me develop and confirm many of the ideas in this book, and they have provided me with new leads for conducting my ongoing research. Most of all, they have encouraged me by their applause, their positive laughter, and their personal expressions to me that what I was telling them or suggesting to them was making a difference in their lives.

I especially acknowledge my boyhood friend Paul Heacock, who made many useful and practical suggestions for making this book more readable.

Another person without whose help this book would not have been possible is Jim Hatleli. Jim took my handwritten manuscript and set it up on a computer. I cannot begin to repay him for the extraordinary amount of time he devoted to this project.

Finally, to my family—my wife, Dana, and my sons, Scott and Steven—I say thank you for standing behind me through life's ups and downs. They have had to endure my moods daily. I appreciate their understanding of my need to stay fully focused on this endeavor. And now I am prepared to fully share the fruits of my labor with them. I hope to show Scott and Steven that hard work does indeed pay off.

CHAPTER 1

Focusing on the Payoff

Productivity: Payoff and Results

#1

Concentrate on the payoffs that result from effective productivity.

The key to greater productivity is to work as often as you can on the things that give you the highest payoff. What is important is to be proactive and cognitive. That is, think before doing and decide each day what will give you and those around you the greatest payoff. These are the activities that deserve your time. This applies both at work and at home. The following Productivity Paradigm puts this concept into perspective.

Productivity Paradigm

3. Procrastination • Fear of risk • Ineffective problem solving/decision making • Lack of training • Lack of or unclear delegation	**4. Gratification (Productivity Power)** • Goal-oriented • Visionary • Climate of motivation • Clear communication • Enough resources • Effective leadership
1. Demotivation • Lack of motivating climate • Lack of leadership • Unclear or no direction/goals	**2. Rationalization** • Conflict over what is high payoff • Lack of or ineffective communication • Lack of resources • Constantly changing priorities

High → Low on vertical axis labeled **PAYOFF (*vision)**

Horizontal axis: Low ◄— Results-oriented —► High

*Vision: a clear definition of important goals and tasks

1. **DEMOTIVATION**: Low payoff (vision); low results-oriented. These individuals continually work on low-payoff activities that yield low results—many times because the individuals don't have a clear vision of what is important. The bottom left quadrant of the paradigm lists some of the symptoms of the demotivated person. Those who are in this mode are consumed by the ordinary. They may work long hours, but they never seem to accomplish very much that is important. They become frustrated and demotivated because they aren't getting any payoffs such as recognition or a sense of accomplishment.

2. **RATIONALIZATION**: Low payoff (vision); high results-oriented. The bottom right quadrant shows some of the symptoms of rationalization behavior. The parties involved conflict over what is important, so they aren't working in tandem. Although they may be results-oriented, they may well be focused on the wrong things. They rationalize that they are making progress. Supervisors and employees often cause and experience this problem because of ineffective communication, lack of resources, or constantly changing priorities.

3. **PROCRASTINATION**: High payoff (vision); low results-oriented. Procrastinators know what is important, but they put off following through for various reasons. They procrastinate because they may fear failure. They may not be able to make decisions or solve problems effectively. Sometimes people don't follow through because they don't know how to do the work. They haven't been properly trained. Sometimes the work isn't delegated properly or the "delegatee" is given responsibility but no authority to make decisions.

4. **GRATIFICATION**: High payoff (vision); high results-oriented. These are people who have productivity power. They can be supervisors, employees, homemakers, small business owners, and others who have a clear vision of the future. They are goal-oriented and work to achieve their goals (high payoff). They take action. They are self-motivated and motivating to others. They can clearly communicate their vision so that others want to follow. They consistently accomplish their goals and tasks that yield high payoffs.

Identifying Your Payoff Activities

YOU TRY IT!

Exercise 1: What are the payoffs that are important to you?

AT WORK	AT HOME
_____	_____
_____	_____
_____	_____
_____	_____
_____	_____
_____	_____
_____	_____
_____	_____
_____	_____
_____	_____

Compare your answers with those listed on the next page.

RULE OF PRODUCTIVITY PAYOFF: Always concentrate on some activities each day that will give you high results and high payoff. Discipline yourself to define and follow through on the important tasks.

Therefore:

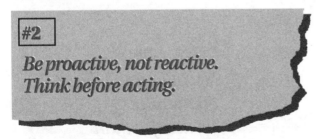

#2

Be proactive, not reactive. Think before acting.

Proactive behavior means thinking before acting. Reactive behavior means acting before thinking.

Ask yourself:

"How can I best use my time and the time of those around me to be most productive at this moment?"

"Productivity comes from commitment, not from authority."

W. L. Gore

Some of the payoffs that people strive for (according to seminar participants):

AT WORK

✓ Recognition

✓ More discretionary time (to work on other important activities)

✓ Less stress (As you finish a job, you bring it to closure.)

✓ More money

✓ Getting the boss off my back (That is usually the way it is stated. A more positive way to say it is "earning the boss's respect and trust.")

✓ Other *challenging* work (The key word here is *challenging.* People like challenging work but very much resent taking on more work for the sake of taking on more work. Unfortunately, sometimes the reward for doing a good job is just more work. That's not a payoff.)

✓ Promotions

✓ Greater productivity

✓ Quality work

✓ More customers (Customers like it when businesses deliver. If a business does, customers come back. The real payoff is that the customer keeps the business in business. Thus, you have a job.)

AT HOME

✓ More leisure time

✓ A balanced life

✓ Happiness

✓ Peace of mind (You accomplished important things at work, so at home you can relax.)

✓ Time to spend with spouse (or partner) and children

✓ To like your job better, rather than resenting it

✓ More time for hobbies

✓ More time to spend with friends

✓ To feel good about self (self-esteem, self-satisfaction)

"I would rather have 30 minutes of wonderful than a lifetime of nothing special."

(Shelby, from the play *Steel Magnolias*)

From Zadig, A Mystery of Fate:
by Voltaire

What, of all things in the world, is the longest and the shortest, the swiftest and the slowest, the most divisible and the most extended, the most neglected and the most regretted without which nothing can be done, which devours all that is little, and enlivens all that is great?

Time.

Nothing is longer, since it is the measure of eternity.

Nothing is shorter, since it is insufficient for the accomplishment of your projects.

Nothing is more slow to him that expects, nothing more rapid to him that enjoys.

In greatness it extends to infinity, in smallness it is infinitely divisible.

All men neglect it; all regret the loss of it; nothing can be done without it.

It consigns to oblivion whatever is unworthy of being transmitted to posterity, and it immortalizes such actions as are truly great.

Time is man's most precious asset.

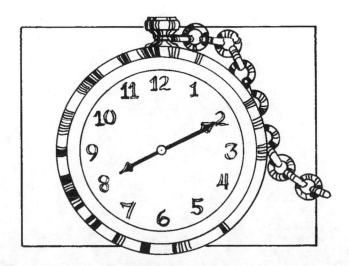

CHAPTER 2

Defining Your Productivity Payoffs

The Concept of Important Versus Urgent

#3

Everything that is urgent is not necessarily the most important.

Consider both importance and urgency when deciding what to act on. Sometimes we believe everything is important and try to accomplish three or four tasks simultaneously. The result is that nothing gets completed. It is important to define which tasks are most important and urgent for you to accomplish now (or in the near future) and to work on each task, one at a time.

Before you begin working each day, give yourself a priority analysis. Exercise 2 explains how.

YOU TRY IT!

Exercise 2: Priority Analysis

1. List your top five or six priorities for the day in the first column.

2. In the second column, rank your priorities with 1 being most important.

3. Next, consider which priority is most urgent for you to begin and to complete. Use a weighted value of 1, 2, or 3, with 1 being the most urgent, for each of your priorities.

4. Multiply the importance factor by the urgency factor for each priority. The fourth column will show a raw score for each item.

5. In the fifth column, rank your priorities from low score to high score. The lowest score becomes your highest priority. If you have a tie, that is, the same raw score for two or more items, then subjectively choose one over the other so that you ultimately have priorities 1 through 6.

Performing this simple daily exercise will give you a clear idea of what you need to accomplish each day.

Today's Priorities	Rank Value Importance (with "1" being *most* important)	X	Time Value 1=Urgent, most important 2=Important, needs to be done 3=Important, but can wait		Raw Score	Priorities In order from low score to high
_____	_____	X	_____	=	_____	_____
_____	_____	X	_____	=	_____	_____
_____	_____	X	_____	=	_____	_____
_____	_____	X	_____	=	_____	_____
_____	_____	X	_____	=	_____	_____
_____	_____	X	_____	=	_____	_____

The Concept of Success—
Getting Meaningful Results

#4

$I \times U = S^2$

*Importance x urgency =
success or stress*

> *"The world little
> knows or cares how
> many storms the ship
> met at sea. It only
> wants to know did
> the captain bring the
> ship safely to port."*
>
> (stated in a speech presented by
> LaSalle Leffall, M.D.)

The formula in Idea #4 is a symbolic formula. That is, it doesn't have mathematical relevance, but it does express a basic concept for achieving greater productivity.

> *"I studied the lives of
> great men and famous
> women; and I found that
> the men and women
> who got to the top were
> those who did the jobs
> they had in hand, with
> everything they had of
> energy, enthusiasm, and
> hard work."*
>
> Harry Truman

What you are striving for is success through meaningful results. If you consider everything to be equally important and equally urgent, you will probably experience *stress* rather than success. You will work on everything and finish nothing. Therefore, you will have a lack of closure—lots of loose ends that can make you very stressful.

Remember S^2 stands for the extremes, success and stress. Success is related to being proactive; stress is related to being reactive.

Reactive   Proactive

←————————————————————————————————→

STRESS   SUCCESS

By thinking first, you are more likely to work in an organized manner rather than in a chaotic, reactive way.

What Is Success?

It means different things to different people. It usually is whatever you consider the payoff to be.

Here is a universal definition of success:

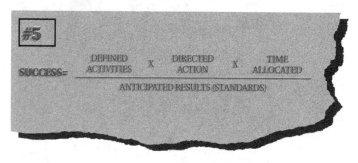

Translated, this formula means that first you identify what needs to be accomplished (as you did in the Priority Analysis in Exercise 2). But just defining your priority activities won't make you successful.

You must take directed, targeted action. That means you must have a daily plan, a system for working on one thing at a time. In the formula, "time allocated" is the specific block of time you designate to accomplish your tasks or activities.

Each task should have standards, or goals and objectives. You can probably rush through a job and get it done. In fact, you may be able to accomplish several activities. But if they are done haphazardly, without quality, you may not be successful in the long run. It is important to divide a priority job into meaningful activities with standards for accomplishing them.

Ralph Waldo Emerson's definition of success

To laugh often and much;

To win the respect of intelligent people and the affection of children;

To earn the appreciation of honest critics and endure the betrayal of false friends;

To appreciate beauty,

To find the best in others;

To leave the world a bit better, whether by a healthy child, a garden patch or a redeemed social condition;

To know that even one life has breathed easier because you have lived.

This is to have succeeded.

Taking Action for Success

Here is an example of the practical application of the formula for success:

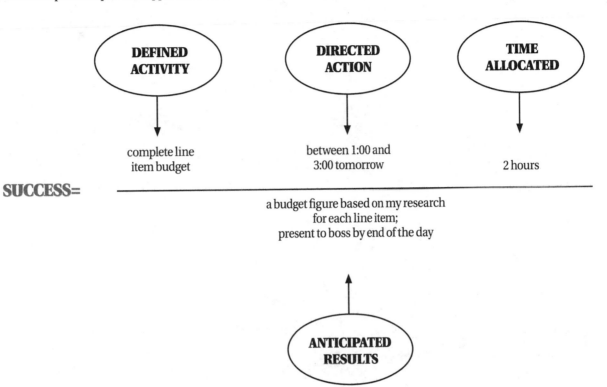

SUCCESS=

In this example, the success (or end result) is presenting a well-researched and quality line item budget to the boss by the end of the next day, to meet the boss's deadline. If the boss accepts the budget, that is one of the payoffs. Another payoff is closure—you don't need to worry any more about completing the activity.

> "Success is turning knowledge into positive action."
>
> Dorothy Leeds

CHAPTER 3

Working on the Right Things

> *"There are many days when you feel like the javelin competitor who won the toss of the coin and elected to receive."*
>
> Ed Meese

How to Set Priorities

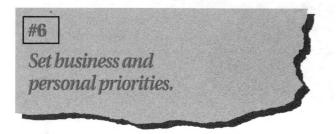

#6

*Set business and
personal priorities.*

Use I x U = S² to:

1. Set work priorities each day.
2. Set work priorities each week.
3. Define your personal priorities each day and/or for the weekend.
4. Determine long-term work priorities.

It is important to have a long-term idea of what your priorities should be. Long-term means different things to different people. But in terms of setting priorities, consider long-term to be your defined priorities for at least the next six months.

Exercise 3 will show you how to use $I \times U = S^2$ to set your long-term work priorities (for the next six months) to stay focused on productivity and payoff.

YOU TRY IT!

Exercise 3: Setting Long-term Priorities

Priorities for the next six months	Rank Value Importance (with "1" being *most* important)	X	Time Value 1=Urgent, most important 2=Important, needs to be done 3=Important, but can wait	Raw Score	Priorities In order from low score to high*
_____	_____	X	_____ =	_____	_____
_____	_____	X	_____ =	_____	_____
_____	_____	X	_____ =	_____	_____
_____	_____	X	_____ =	_____	_____
_____	_____	X	_____ =	_____	_____
_____	_____	X	_____ =	_____	_____

*If you have a tie, subjectively choose one priority over the other so that your priorities are ranked 1 to 6.

Share your list of long-term priorities with your supervisor. Come to an agreement about what is payoff. If you don't, you could end up in the "rationalization " mode defined in Chapter 1.

You may have to give up a couple of your priorities in favor of your supervisor's. That's OK. At least you will have a common under standing of what is payoff for the next six months, and will therefore be more productive. However, don't give up all of your priority items in favor of your supervisor's or you will be frustrated. (See Chapter 15 for ways to negotiate with your boss.).

Staying Goal Focused

There are two kinds of activities: Job description and goal-related.

#7

Realize that job description duties are often low payoff with little results. Get them done, but focus your attention on the high-payoff goal-related activities.

Job description: These are routine duties that quite often have low payoffs. Sometimes these duties are defined as system-imposed, nondiscretionary, or routine activities. If you have a job description, look at the last item. It probably reads "… and other duties as assigned." If you spend the majority of your work life doing "other duties as assigned," you will likely end up at either extreme on the following continuum.

RUST OUT
(boredom—too much work with little meaning and lack of challenge)

BURN OUT
(too much work with little payoff)

Goal-related: These are usually high-payoff activities directly related to your goals and your organization's goals; thus, they yield meaningful results. Focusing on them gives you productivity power. (See the Productivity Paradigm in Chapter 1, high results, high-payoff activities.)

Here are some examples of job description and goal-related activities.

JOB DESCRIPTION (ROUTINE)

✓ Most meetings
✓ Most phone calls
✓ People interruptions
✓ Most mail (the time needed to read or scan it)
✓ Most reports

(*Note:* Consider the word *most* in the Job Description column. Some meetings, phone calls, people interruptions, and reports are constructive. Some mail is important. But we have a tendency to spend too much time on these activities.)

GOAL-RELATED (HIGH PAYOFF)

✓ Contacting your customers
✓ Preparing marketing materials
✓ Training and development
✓ Career planning
✓ Selling

"What can be done at anytime is never done at all."

English Proverb

Integrating Goal-related and Job Description Activities

 #8

Work on job description and goal-related activities each day.

Even though job description priorities are often low yield, they must get done. And, unfortunately, they will consume the majority of your day. According to the 80-20 rule, we spend about 80 percent of our day working on job description activities that yield only 20 percent results.

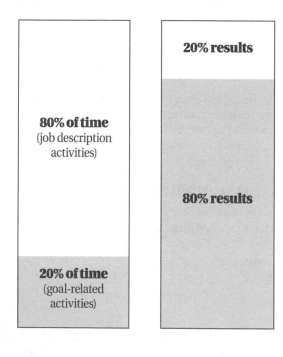

20% results

80% of time
(job description activities)

80% results

20% of time
(goal-related activities)

#9

Schedule time for high-payoff activities.

Closely monitor and scrutinize the other 20 percent of your time so you can work on goal-related activities. These yield the biggest payoff and greatest productivity— about 80 percent. But we don't automatically work on goal-related activities. We must commit to them. It is important to schedule time each day for your high-payoff, results-oriented, goal-related priorities.

#10

As you move up in an organization, you will probably have even less than 20 percent of your time to devote to goal-related activities. Use it wisely.

When you manage others, you will need to:

- Spend more time with them. But that can work to your advantage. (See Chapter 10.)
- Answer their questions and provide direction.
- Delegate to them. That takes time, but it's worth it. (See Chapter 18.)
- Follow up with them to be sure they are productive.
- Help them set goals.
- Evaluate their performance.

Using Discretionary Time

#11

The time that you have left each day to devote to goal-related, more productive activities is called discretionary time.

Discretion means judgment. Here, it refers to using your good judgment with the 20 percent of the day that is yours—using your personal power to be proactive about your daily choices for productivity.

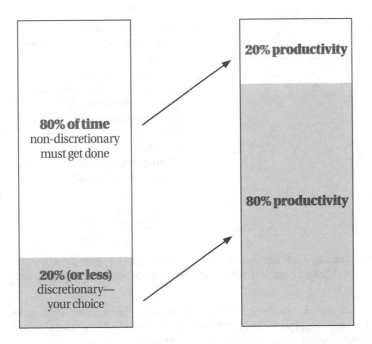

80% of time
non-discretionary
must get done

20% (or less)
discretionary—
your choice

20% productivity

80% productivity

"I am only one, but I am someone. I can't do everything, but I can do something."

(Quoted in a speech by Mrs. Marlin Perkins)

Being Efficient and Effective to Achieve Excellence

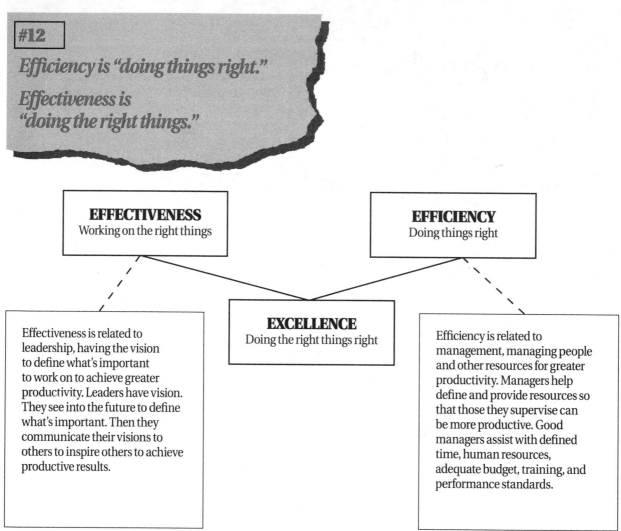

#12

Efficiency is "doing things right."

Effectiveness is "doing the right things."

EFFECTIVENESS
Working on the right things

EFFICIENCY
Doing things right

EXCELLENCE
Doing the right things right

Effectiveness is related to leadership, having the vision to define what's important to work on to achieve greater productivity. Leaders have vision. They see into the future to define what's important. Then they communicate their visions to others to inspire others to achieve productive results.

Efficiency is related to management, managing people and other resources for greater productivity. Managers help define and provide resources so that those they supervise can be more productive. Good managers assist with defined time, human resources, adequate budget, training, and performance standards.

You can be a leader and manager of both yourself and others by working efficiently and effectively. By doing the right things, you can achieve excellence. Remember that excellence is different from perfection. Perfectionism behavior is procrastination behavior. (See Chapter 14.)

You don't need to be a formal leader or manager to apply the concepts of effectiveness and efficiency. Learn to set an example for others by being your own best leader and manager. That is, lead yourself. Have a vision of where and what you want to be in the future. Then manage in the present to reach the future by getting the resources you need to achieve success.

CHAPTER 4

Planning: Defining the Future

Being Results-oriented

#13

Don't just work. Spend your time working on the right things.

HOURS WORKED MEASURES INPUT; RESULTS MEASURE OUTPUT.

The number of hours you devote to work isn't as important as working on the right things. You can come into work early, stay late, work through your lunch, and work eighty hours a week. But the time you spend at work doesn't necessarily equal productivity. Working long hours doesn't guarantee that you will have any greater productivity or achieve anything more than the person who works forty to fifty hours a week, but who works on the right things—the high-payoff activities. If you really want to be productive and successful and get positive results, it is important to learn to *plan*.

- **Your life**
- **Your year**
- **Your next quarter**
- **Your week**
- **Your day**

Then devote a part of each day—up to 20 percent—to work toward high-payoff activities based on your planned vision. It would be nice to spend more than 20 percent of your time on these activities. Unfortunately, though, your job description activities will beckon you.

> *"If there is somewhere you want to go, you must believe that you have already arrived."*
>
> Richard Bach in *Jonathan Livingston Seagull*

Being results-oriented and striving for the payoff

Dale Carnegie told a story about two men who were out chopping wood. One man worked hard all day, took no breaks, and only stopped briefly for lunch.

The other chopper took several breaks during the day and a short nap at lunch. At the end of the day, the woodsman who had taken no breaks was quite disturbed to see that the other chopper had cut more wood than he had. He said, "I don't understand. Every time I looked around, you were sitting down, yet you cut more wood than I did."

His companion asked, "Did you also notice that while I was sitting down, I was sharpening my ax?"

Source: Joe Griffith. *Speaker's Library Of Business Stories, Anecdotes and Humor.* Englewood Cliffs, NJ: Prentice Hall, 1990

Learning to Plan

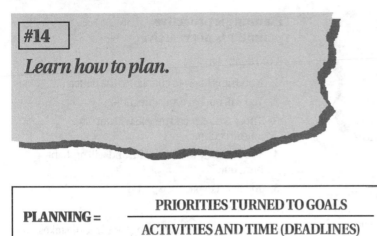

#14

Learn how to plan.

"You've got to be very careful if you don't know where you are going, because you might get there."

Yogi Berra

PLANNING = $\dfrac{\text{PRIORITIES TURNED TO GOALS}}{\text{ACTIVITIES AND TIME (DEADLINES)}}$

What planning means:

1. Priorities are wishes and hopes. They are stated in powerless terms.
2. Goals are action statements. They are stated in powerful language.
3. Each goal must be broken down into activities that have deadlines.
4. Then you need to take action.
5. Each activity must be completed. This is closure.
   As you bring closure to an activity, you get closer to the ultimate achievement of your goal.

Consider this example of a plan to go back to college:

I *hope* to go back to school *someday.*
I *wish* I could get started soon.
(Powerless)

I plan to go back to school in September (year) to complete my bachelor's degree in business administration by June (year). (Powerful)

PLANNING = $\dfrac{\text{PRIORITIES TURNED TO GOALS}}{\text{ACTIVITIES AND TIME (DEADLINES)}}$

- To save x amount of money for school by (deadline date).
- To select my classes by (deadline date).
- To have my schedule set by (deadline date).
- To make baby-sitting arrangements by (deadline date).
- To discuss a change in work hours with my supervisor by (deadline date).

Defining Your Future

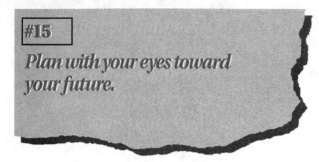

#15

Plan with your eyes toward your future.

Planning is your road map for getting from the present to your desired future. The primary reason to plan is to get you from where you are to where you want to be. Other reasons to plan are:

- To give direction and focus to a project or to some aspect of your life.
- To keep crises to a minimum.
- To use time more efficiently and effectively.
- To work toward achieving goals rather than relieving tension.
- To achieve other payoffs such as advancement in the organization.

Planning is proactive; planning is not reactive.

If you don't plan:

1. Nothing is likely to change for the better.
2. You will not have any direction.
3. Those who depend on you will not have any direction.
4. You are likely to be stressful and will probably burn out.
5. You won't experience payoff.

And:

6. You will likely keep making the same mistakes over and over without looking for solutions and planning your strategy.

Consider this anecdote based on a story by James H. Austin in *Chase, Chance and Creativity:*

One day a doctor had a vision of a long line of patients waiting to see him—a line extending far out of his office and into the street. He already knew what the diagnosis was: Each patient had a sprained ankle from stepping into the deep hole in the sidewalk out in front of the office. The doctor knew the source of his own dilemma. He was just too busy seeing patients in pain with sprained ankles. He never could take the time to go out and repair the sidewalk.

What's the moral of the story?

Take time to plan.

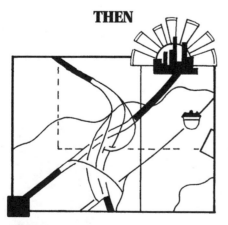

THEN

NOW

"If your ship doesn't come in, swim out to it."

Jonathan Winters

Taking Personal Responsibility

We sometimes believe that if no one tells us what is important, then nothing is important. Too often we rely on others to determine value. As a result, we go through life underachieving and blaming it on others.

#16

Control your environment by taking personal responsibility to plan your future and your outcomes, both in your work life and personal life.

It is up to each of us to plan our own work life and personal life. Don't wait for others to do it for you. But if your supervisor does provide you with meaningful direction, gladly accept it and thank him or her for it.

Remember:

✓ Don't have a "victim mentality" or be an "iffer":

"If they would help me, I'd be more productive."

"If they would give me the resources, I'd perform."

"If it weren't for the traffic, I'd be on time for meetings."

✓ Get started. Take action to define your own goals and goal-related activities.

✓ Negotiate your goals with others who will be affected, including your boss.

✓ Reach agreement and follow through.

Be in control!

"If it is to be, it is up to me."

Ralph Waldo Emerson

Not Taking Personal Responsibility

**Some people just let life happen to them.
They waste time and let life pass them by.**

Here are some of the ways we waste time:

6 months of our lives waiting at stoplights. (Find something meaningful to do. See Chapter 17.)

8 months of our lives opening junk mail. (Get control of the mail. See Chapter 13.)

1 year of our lives trying to find lost objects. (Get organized. See Chapter 13.)

2 years of our lives returning phone calls. (Take control of the telephone. See Chapter 11.)

4 years of our lives doing housework. (Decide how you can streamline it, delegate it, or pay someone to do it so that you can concentrate on high-payoff activities.)

5 years of our lives waiting in lines. (Take personal responsibility to arrive where you are going early enough to avoid long lines. Always look at alternatives.)

6 years of our lives eating. (That's OK. We need the fuel to energize ourselves for all the payoff activities we're working on. Just be sure you are eating the right things. See Chapter 19.)

Source: Study conducted by Priority Management Pittsburgh, Inc.

Moral:

**Don't just let life happen to you. Take personal
responsibility to take control. Set goals to get
around life's obstacles. Be proactive.**

> *"It is not enough to be busy;
> so are ants. The question is:
> What are we busy about?"*
>
> Thoreau

Take Charge of Your Life

The Road Not Taken

Two roads diverged in a yellow wood,
And sorry I could not travel both
And be one traveler, long I stood
And looked down one as far as I could
To where it bent in the undergrowth;

Then took the other, as just as fair,
And having perhaps the better claim,
because it was grassy and wanted wear;
Though as for that the passing there
Had worn them really about the same,

And both that morning equally lay
In leaves no step had trodden black.
Oh, I kept the first for another day!
Yet knowing how way leads on to way,
I doubted if I should ever come back.

I shall be telling this with a sigh
Somewhere ages and ages hence:
Two roads diverged in a wood, and I—
I took the one less traveled by,
And that has made all the difference.

Robert Frost

CHAPTER 5

Setting "Real" Work and Personal Goals

> "Give me a stock clerk with a goal and I will give you a man who will make history. Give me a man without a goal and I will give you a stock clerk."
>
> J.C. Penney

Concentrating on Goals

> **#17**
>
> *Cut through the daily obstacles and the routine by being focused.*

> **#18**
>
> *View goals as a means to an end, not as an end in themselves.*

How to keep focused:

- Keep your goals before you visually (on a bulletin board, in a digital file, on your desk or desktop).
- Work on them daily to achieve results.
- Review them weekly to track your progress.

Obstacles are what you see when you take your eyes off of your goals.

Simply knowing your goals won't help you achieve them. You must act on them to achieve productivity power. In other words, you must turn your knowledge into action.

Knowledge ⟶ Action

But here's what often happens when an organization tries to set specific goals:

- Someone attends a seminar and learns the importance of goal setting.
- This person goes back to work and sends out a memo to everyone in the company to prepare a list of 10 to 15 goals and to turn the list in to the secretary by 3:00 p.m. on Friday. The memo also includes a list of "suggested" goals.
- Everyone (well, almost everyone) compiles a list of goals by the 3:00 p.m. Friday deadline.
- The secretary assembles them into one master file and prints them out.
- All the goals are collated and bound into a booklet that says "Goals: Acme Corporation."
- Everyone goes back to what they were doing before.

This process goes on all the time in organizations. Goals are forced on people. The employees lack commitment to achieve the goals because the goals aren't really theirs. What's more, no accountability is built into the process. Employees don't receive feedback. Those who are struggling don't receive direction. Those who do achieve aren't recognized. The process is demotivating. (See the Productivity Paradigm in Chapter 1.) Sometime later, usually in about a year, management formally "evaluates" employees on these goals—goals for which they received no feedback or direction. You can guess the outcome: lack of commitment and, therefore, lack of accomplishment.

The Traits of Action Goals

#19

Set ACTION goals.

Here are the characteristics of action goals:

Are measurable

> If a goal is not measurable, then it is probably just a wish or a hope.

Compatible with your mission

> If a goal is not compatible with your company, department, or life mission, then it will probably result in low payoff because it is likely an unimportant goal.

Time-specific

> Each of your goals should have a start time and a finish date. Without both, you may lack the commitment to follow through.

In writing

> If you put your goal in writing, it will probably be more clear, and you can communicate it and share it with others. Writing out your goals makes them visual. A written goal is more likely to have been thought out and, therefore, there is a greater chance you will accomplish it.

Ownership and accountability

> Goals must be owned by those who set them and by others vested with the responsibility for carrying them out. In other words, everyone involved must agree that the goals are important and useful. Those involved are more likely to take ownership if they participate in setting the goals.

Negotiated (agreed upon)

> If you and others who are involved (your supervisor or employees or family) reach agreement about what the goals should be and how they should be accomplished, then there is likely to be commitment to follow through. If there is disagreement, disharmony, and unresolved conflict about the goals, people will "do their own thing" and rationalize that it is the "right thing to do." They will likely receive little payoff. (See the Productivity Paradigm in Chapter 1.)

The Importance of Setting Personal Goals

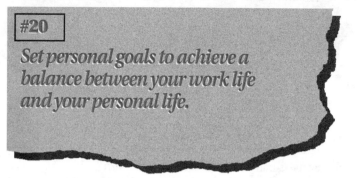

#20

Set personal goals to achieve a balance between your work life and your personal life.

Everything that's been discussed so far in this book about being productive applies to your personal life as well as to your business life. Isn't it true that if you're not happy in your personal life, you probably won't do well at work? Therefore, it's very important to define what's important for you to accomplish away from work.

"Anywhere is paradise."

George Harrison

"Many people aim at nothing and hit it with amazing accuracy."

Anonymous

Consider setting goals in these areas of your personal life:

PERSONAL DEVELOPMENT

What do you want to be when you grow up—no matter how old you are now? If you are where you want to be, what do you need to do to stay there?

Example: I will take a community college course in creative writing beginning in January (year) and complete it within three months.

I will also attend three business seminars between March 1 and December 31.

MARRIAGE/FAMILY

What specific goals do you have for spending quality time with those who are close to you? Have you scheduled a vacation? Do you go out to dinner together? Do you enjoy cultural events together?

Example: Our family will take a vacation to Cape Cod between August 1 and August 15.

My spouse (or partner) and I will attend at least two movies each month for the next 10 months.

SOCIAL/FRIENDS

Do you plan specific events or outings with friends on a regular basis? Do you call them rather than wait around hoping they will call you?

Example: I will invite at least one friend or couple to our home for dinner at least once a month for the next six months.

FINANCIAL

Do you have a financial plan to save and invest money, even if it is only $5 a week? How disciplined are you to follow a financial plan?

Example: I will save $25 a week for the next year. Then I'll reevaluate my financial situation and either increase or decrease the amount I'm saving.

PHYSICAL

How well do you take care of yourself physically? Do you follow an exercise program? Do you have a dietary plan?

Example: On October 1, I will begin a walking/jogging program for a half hour a day, four days a week and continue it through September 31.

SPIRITUAL

What do you believe in? Do you have a religious affiliation? Are you taking steps to define one if you desire?

Example: I'll attend religious services each week for the next six months.

COMMUNITY/VOLUNTEER SERVICE

What organizations do you help out either physically or financially? How much time do you spend in charitable or volunteer pursuits?

Example: I will do community volunteer work for at least two hours a week for the next year with the following organizations:

_____

_____

_____

Rules for Setting Personal Goals

Here are some guidelines to follow as you set personal goals:

#21

Set goals only for the areas of your life where you feel a sense of commitment.

#22

Choose no more than five personal goals. It is unrealistic to try to accomplish more than that and still carry out your routine and ordinary responsibilities.

#23

Use action goal statements to write out the specific personal goals you would like to achieve.

Remember, goals must be specific and measurable. Don't wait until it's too late to set personal goals!

In the 1960s, Art Linkletter had a segment on his *House Party* show called "Kids Say the Darndest Things." Linkletter wrote books related to the responses children gave to questions he would ask them on the show.

One time when he asked kids to define "love," he got answers like "When mom takes me to a movie" or "When dad plays baseball with me."

At the end of the show, Linkletter said, "Children define love as the time spent with them."

We all have family—parents, children, spouses, and others. Have you set personal goals for spending quality time with them?

In a recent Gallup poll, only 41 percent of the respondents indicated they had planned the job they held at the time. Nearly 65 percent said they would change careers if they could, and almost a third expected to change jobs within three years. And according to a Marriott Senior's Attitude Survey, adults over 65 years of age indicated they would have changed these areas of their lives:

What seniors (over 65) would have changed in their lives

(Respondents could choose more than one):

Saved more money	**51%**
Traveled more	**47%**
Chosen a different career	**31%**
Lived somewhere else	**18%**
Gotten married/married someone else	**11%**

Moral:

Set a personal goal to become what you want to be. Don't leave your job and your personal life to chance.

YOU TRY IT!

Exercise 4: Enjoying Life Through Positive Action

Write at least one action goal statement for the following personal categories that interest you or you feel committed to.

✓ Personal Development

_____
_____
_____

✓ Marriage/Family

_____
_____
_____

✓ Social/Friends

_____
_____
_____

✓ Financial

_____
_____
_____

✓ Physical

_____
_____
_____

✓ Spiritual

_____
_____
_____

✓ Community/Volunteer Service

_____
_____
_____

✓ Other

_____
_____
_____
_____

Take Time

Take time to think,

It is the source of power.

Take time to play,

It is the secret of perpetual youth.

Take time to read,

It is the fountain of wisdom.

Take time to love and be loved,

It is a privilege.

Take time to be friendly,

It is the road to happiness.

Take time to laugh,

It is the music of the soul.

Take time to give,

It is too short a day to be selfish.

Take time to work,

It is the price of success.

Take time to pray,

It is the greatest power on Earth.

Author Unknown

CHAPTER 6

Strategic Planning for Targeted Productivity

> "We cannot discover new oceans unless we have the courage to lose sight of the shore."
>
> E. E. Cummings

Defining Strategic Planning

#24

Concentrate on strategic planning to help you define the objectives, activities, and deadlines for each of your goals.

"When you fail to plan, you plan to fail."

Dr. Robert Schuller

The process of strategic planning

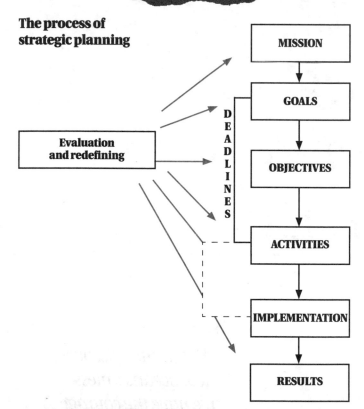

Answers the question "why?":
- Why are we in business?
- Why does my department exist? (Mission statements are broad and general.)

Answers the question "what?":
- What are we trying to achieve in relation to our mission? (Goals are specific. See the qualities of action goals in Chapter 5.)

Answers the question "how?":
- How are we going to accomplish our goals?
- There is likely more than one objective per goal. There are usually a series of "hows" to reach a goal. (Objectives are specific, much like goals.)

Answers several questions—"who," "when," "where," "how," "how much?":
- The activities are the details necessary for accomplishing each objective. These activities are sometimes delegated to other people. (See Chapter 18 on delegation.)

Answers the question "when?":
- When will we implement the strategic plan?
- Instead of putting the goal and strategic plan away, the goal is immediately implemented according to the plan's timetable or deadlines.

- Measuring quantifiable aspects of the goals to determine whether you achieved success.

#25

It is important to continually evaluate the relevance of your mission and strategies.

In their book *In Search of Excellence*, Tom Peters and Robert Waterman, Jr., refer to this continual evaluation as MBWA—Management By Walking Around. In other words, you are always observing the process to be sure that you are succeeding and that the plan is still relevant.

Here's an example of the strategic planning process:

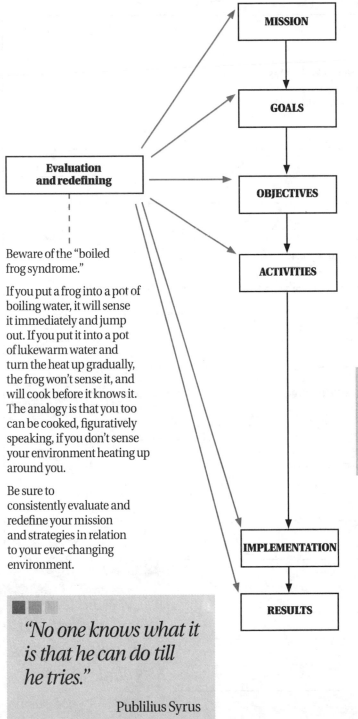

Evaluation and redefining

Beware of the "boiled frog syndrome."

If you put a frog into a pot of boiling water, it will sense it immediately and jump out. If you put it into a pot of lukewarm water and turn the heat up gradually, the frog won't sense it, and will cook before it knows it. The analogy is that you too can be cooked, figuratively speaking, if you don't sense your environment heating up around you.

Be sure to consistently evaluate and redefine your mission and strategies in relation to your ever-changing environment.

Why?
(Why are you in business?)
• To build the best widgets in the industry, concentrating on quality, and to provide our customers with the best possible customer service so that we keep their business. (Broad, general statement—not usually measurable)

What?
(What are we trying to achieve in relation to our mission?)
• To increase our customer base by 10 percent by December 31 (year). (Your company very likely has several goals. Notice that this goal is measurable and has a deadline.)

How?
(How are we going to accomplish our goals?)
• By developing a customer service training program for front line and middle management employees by March 1 (year). (There are probably several objectives related to each goal.)
• Who will do the training and who are we training?
• When will the training take place and how frequently?
• Where will we conduct the training that is convenient and conducive to learning?
• How will the course content look and who will develop it?
• How much will these activities cost?

#26

There must be deadlines for every phase of activity.

When?
(When will we implement the strategic plan?)
• By April 1 (year).

• To be determined by whether or not we reach our quantifiable goal of a 10 percent increase in our customer base.

"No one knows what it is that he can do till he tries."

Publilius Syrus

Defining Your Strategies

YOU TRY IT!

Exercise 5: Developing a Strategic Plan
Develop a strategic plan for just one of your personal or work-related goals.

| MISSION | Why? (Why is your company or department in business? Or, what is your mission in life?) |

_____

_____

_____

_____

| GOALS | What? (Write out just one action goal statement.) |

_____

_____

_____

_____

| OBJECTIVES | How? (Write out one objective to help you achieve your goal. Realize that you may have several objectives.) |

_____

_____

_____

_____

| ACTIVITIES |

Who? _____

When? _____

Where?_____

How? _____

How much? $ _____

> *"The will to win is important, but the will to prepare is vital."*
>
> Joe Paterno

A Word of Caution About Strategic Planning

Remember these key points about goal setting and strategic planning:

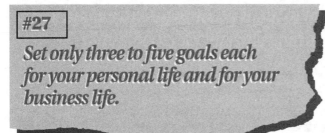

#27

Set only three to five goals each for your personal life and for your business life.

One of the biggest problems with goal-setting is that people become overzealous. They set too many goals and set themselves up for failure. Remember that you have only 20 percent discretionary time, at best, each day to work to achieve your goals.

Caution: If you're a supervisor, don't ask your employees to set more than about three to five goals a year. If you do, you likely will set them up for failure. Of course, the number of goals they should work toward depends on the magnitude of the goals.

Keep your strategic planning process to no more than three to five hours for the five goals you set. Keep the process simple. If you spend more than five hours developing the strategic planning process, you're spending too much time. General rule: spend no more than forty minutes per goal.

Many times, the process of strategic planning becomes an end in itself rather than a means to an end. It works like this:

1. A strategic planning committee is assembled.
2. The committee meets frequently and at great length.
3. Committee members never focus on the payoff. They just concentrate on "something" so that they can say they did their job.
4. After many hours and lots of conflict, the committee publishes its plan.
5. Then, politically, they push it through the ranks.
6. No one will admit that the plan was developed for the sake of having a plan—not to accomplish something meaningful.
7. Upper management adopts the plan.
8. It is assembled in a book with a nice cover.
9. Everyone goes back to what they were doing before.

Making Sure That Plans Get Implemented

#28

Be sure to integrate goal-related activities (from your strategic plans) with your job description activities each day.

Rules to remember:

1. You will likely spend at least 80 percent of each day working on the routine job description activities. Use this time efficiently.

2. You probably will have only about 20 percent of each day (at best) to work on your goal-related activities.

3. List your job description and goal-related activities on your "To Do" list.

4. In some instances, particularly if you are a supervisor, you will delegate activities to someone else. Be sure that you have included time for following up with this person. Add the follow-up to your "To Do" list. (Remember: "Management By Walking Around.")

5. Keep a separate "To Do" list for your personal activities, and integrate personal goals and work-related goals.

"I have always liked bird dogs better than kennel-fed dogs myself—you know, one that will get out and hunt for food rather than sit on his fanny."

Charles E. Wilson

CHAPTER 7

Putting Your Daily Plan Into Action

> "Nothing is work unless you'd rather be doing something else."
>
> George "Papa Bear" Halas

Working on Priorities

#29

Designate a specific time each day for working on your priorities.

Charles Schwab, who was chairman of Bethlehem Steel back in the 1920s, was concerned about his own lack of productivity and that of his management team. So he called on a management consultant named Ivy Lee to advise him on how to become more productive. Lee told him to write down every evening the six most important things he had to do the next day and list them in their order of importance. Lee said, "If it works for you, have your 'men' try it."

Schwab asked how much he owed Lee for the service. Lee suggested that Schwab use the plan for several months and encourage his other management employees to do the same. Lee then said, "Send me a check for whatever you think the advice is worth."

Reportedly, Mr. Schwab sent Ivy Lee a check for $25,000! Keep in mind this was the 1920s. What would that money be worth today? You could probably add another zero. Schwab later stated that this advice—to list your priorities and schedule them in terms of their importance and then to take action—was one of the most valuable lessons he and his managers had learned. And he felt that $25,000 was a small amount to pay relative to the cost savings the company achieved over time through enhanced productivity.

The key is not to prioritize what's on your schedule, but to schedule your priorities.

"People aren't just lucky. Good things happen to them because they're willing to take chances. I don't even want to think about ties ...

If you don't win, you don't win, but at least you have the experience of going for it, of making something useful happen through efforts."

Joe Paterno

Using Your "To Do" List Creatively

#30

Use a creative "To Do" list that indicates the approximate amount of time you will need to complete each task.

Note that the sample "To Do" list in Figure 1 assigns a time estimate for completing each activity. Using time estimates can help you to work in time blocks. You could be thinking, "When will I ever have a four-hour time block?" Maybe never. But you can have four one-hour time blocks. So, activity time estimates can help you to plan.

THINGS TO DO	Approx. amount of time
1. Work on customer service training program guide (JD)	4 hrs.
2. Interview candidates for field representative position (JD)	3 hrs.
3. Prepare for staff meeting (JD)	45 min.
4. Prepare course content for teambuilding seminar (GR)	3 $1/2$ hrs.
5. Call 10 potential clients (JD)	30 min.
6. Prepare and send marketing letter (GR)	1 $1/2$ hrs.
7. Have meeting with advertising agency about new ads (JD)	1 $1/2$ hrs.
8. Make travel arrangements for next month (JD)	45 min.
9. Conduct annual review (JD)	7 hrs.
10. Write four chapters in productivity book (GR)	3 hrs.

Integrate job description activities with goal-related activities:

• Place a "JD" next to activities that are related to your job description.
• Place a "GR" next to activities that are goal-related.
• Choose which JDs and which GRs you will work on each day.

Figure 1. This "To Do" list has only 10 items. A real "To Do" list would probably contain many more. Look at yours.

#31

Analyze your "To Do" list each day.

• What can you delete?
• What can you delegate? (If you are not a manager and can't delegate, then what can you negotiate with a co-worker?)
• Which items will you transfer from your "To Do" list to your daily planner for commitment and follow-through? Pick and choose. You can't accomplish everything in one day.
• Your "To Do" list is in flux. You are always removing activities (when you accomplish them) and adding new ones. Caution: Don't be too excited to remove or check off an activity if you haven't completed it with quality. Work on the activity with an attitude of excellence. Remember that excellence is doing the right things right.

#32

Use a "Daily Planning Calendar" that breaks the day down into hourly time segments and helps you concentrate on both goal-related and job description (routine) activities.

Turning "To Do's" Into Action

#33

Transfer job description and goal-related activities from your "To Do" list to your daily planner each day.

How to Make It Work

#34

Determine what is realistic for you to accomplish each day.

#35

Schedule your priority activities in specific time blocks.

Remember, your daily plan should integrate goal-related and job description activities.

#36

Schedule strategic reserve time (SRT) on your daily schedule.

Strategic reserve time is open time. SRT is necessary to plan for crises.

There will be crises on most days. If you schedule every moment of your day, you are not being realistic. Build in strategic reserve time.

Be flexible enough to reschedule a time block of activity if you are hit with a crisis.

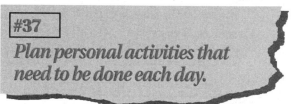

	7:00		**Date**
8:00 }	8:00-9:30-Meet with Tom Wilson,
9:00 }	advertising agency about
	newspaper ads – his office
	SRT
10:00 }	Prepare for staff meeting
11:00 }	Return phone calls
	SRT
12:00 }	Meet with Regional Director –
1:00 }	Pepe's Restaurant
	SRT
2:00 }	Prepare course content for
3:00 }	teambuilding seminar
	SRT
3:00 }	3:00-4:00 Staff meeting
4:00 }
	SRT
5:00 }	Open mail, write one chapter in
7:00 }	"productivity" book

Things To Do	Time

PHONE CALLS
Mary Gilbert
1. Goals
2. Finances
Tom Foreman
1. Staff changes
John Williams
1. Book
2. Car
3. Meeting - Feb. 2
Lorraine Harris
1. Status of Jane's project
2. Correspondence to Acme

MEETINGS
12:00-1:00-Meet with Regional Director
3:00-4:00-Staff meeting

CORRESPONDENCES
1. Follow-up thank you letters from Annual Meeting
2. Memo about real estate and building plan
3. Letters to clients about special promotions

Personal/Family
• Get car washed-11:45 a.m.
• Go to cleaners
• Dept. Store – shoe sale

Other
• Open mail
• Call Mary- tell her happy birthday

Figure 2. Each day, transfer activities from your "To Do" list to your daily planner. Compare the items on the "To Do" list in Figure 1 to the activities listed on this planner.

#37

Plan personal activities that need to be done each day.

Do you ever go to work with little notes in your pocket or purse that remind you to pick up bread and milk or to go to the cleaners or to wash the car? And when you go home at night, do you still have the notes but haven't accomplished the activities? Build these personal activities into your daily schedule.

#38

Jot a handwritten agenda next to each of the people you intend to call.

Do you ever play phone tag? Of course you do. You can go for days trying to reach the person you're calling. When you finally reach that person, unless you have an agenda, you may forget to discuss one of the reasons you called. Then you're into phone tag all over again.

Dealing With Crises

#39

Plan for crises each day by using your strategic reserve time appropriately.

You may be thinking that transferring activities from your "To Do" list to your day planner and then carrying them out on schedule is fine for people who don't have a lot of crises to deal with each day. "What about people like me who have crises-oriented jobs where it's just one crises after another. Surely this process won't work for me," you say.

If you have a crisis-oriented job:

#40

Leave lots of strategic reserve time.

Because it's the nature of your job that you will be frequently interrupted, leave most of your day open.

#41

Commit a specific amount of time each day to work on goal-related activities.

Everyone from the secretary to the distribution manager to the housewife to the middle manager to the company president should have goals. However, the nature of your job (crises-oriented or not crises-oriented) will determine how much time you have to devote to your goal-related activities. If you have a crisis-oriented job, you will have no more than 2 percent to 5 percent of your day to devote to goal-related activities.

#42

If you have a crisis-oriented job, work closely with co-workers to free blocks of time for working on goal-related activities.

Have your co-workers cover for you, and you do the same for them. For example, offer to cover the phone today between 3:30 p.m. and 5:00 p.m. and ask your co-workers to do the same for you tomorrow.

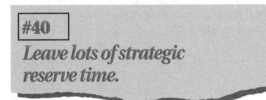

7:00	**Date**	**PHONE CALLS**
8:00 9:00	8:00-9:00-Work on new tracking system for complaint calls	
10:00 11:00		
12:00 1:00		**MEETINGS**
2:00 3:00		
4:00 5:00	4:00-5:00-Continue work on new tracking system for complaint calls	**CORRESPONDENCES**
6:00 7:00		

| Personal/Family | Other |
| • Buy present for Tom | • Open mail
• Turn in physicians' report |

Figure 3. Leave most of your day free to deal with crises if your job demands it, but try to set aside some time for goal-related activities.

Be careful not to be eaten alive by crises!

Have you ever been bitten by an elephant? Probably not. How about a mosquito? Probably so. You see, it's the little things that eat you alive. Don't be consumed by the mosquitoes. Follow your daily plan to carry out your job description and goal-related activities.

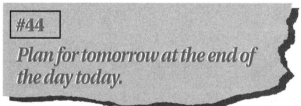

#43

If you have a crisis-oriented job and you are not a crisis-oriented person, set a goal to look for a new job that agrees more with your personality.

"A diamond is a chunk of coal that made good under pressure."

Joe Griffith

If you don't, guess what is likely to happen to you? Burnout!

Be proactive, not reactive. Do something about the situation. Begin looking around now for a new job. Maybe you can transfer to another department in your own company.

If you don't begin looking now, you may have to be reactive later. You could become distraught and start searching frantically. Or, your productivity could go down and you may be asked to leave.

Don't misconstrue this advice. You shouldn't run away from your responsibilities and problems by leaving your job. Consider transferring if your personality is not suited to the crisis-orientation of your job.

When Is the Best Time to Plan?

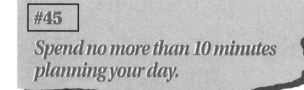

#44

Plan for tomorrow at the end of the day today.

#45

Spend no more than 10 minutes planning your day.

Why? Because you bring closure to today—you are prepared when you go to work tomorrow. And sometimes sleeping on your problems and concerns helps you to consider problems and decisions more efficiently.

Planning each day will likely yield at least one hour more of productivity each day. If you have one more productive hour each day, 365 days per year, you will have an additional 45 eight-hour days. This is called the 13 ½-month calendar.

Choosing a Day Planner

#46

*Set a goal to buy a day planner—
printed, digital or mobile app—
that meets your needs.*

Tom Seaver: *"Hey, Yogi, what
time is it?"*
Yogi Berra: *"You mean now?"*

Common features of printed day planners:

- They all break the day down into
  one-hour segments.
- They come in sizes ranging from desktop to
  pocket size.
- They include an alphabetical phone log.
- They contain an expense log for recording
  your business expenses.
- They are available in your choice of covers
  (usually vinyl or leather).

More detailed printed planners come with:

- Project management pages to manage your
  important projects.
- Pages for taking meeting notes.
- Pages for recording and tracking ideas that
  pop into your mind while you are driving or
  sitting at your desk.
- "To Do" lists.
- Pages for setting goals.

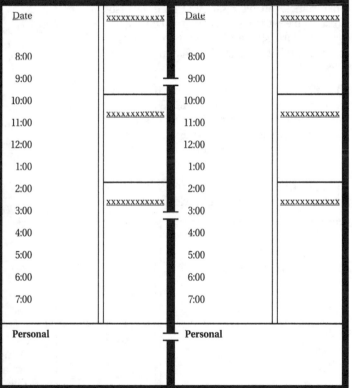

Figure 4. Sample day planner pages (open in center).

*"The next best thing to
knowing something is
knowing where to find it."*

Rupert Murdoch

An assortment of digital planners and mobile phone
applications are now available that provide all the traditional
functions, including scheduling appointments, listing phone
numbers or serving as a tickler file—as well as offering
integration with e-mail, calendars/project management
software, social media and other applications that allow
them to perform numerous other tasks.

Using Your Energy and Checking Your Progress

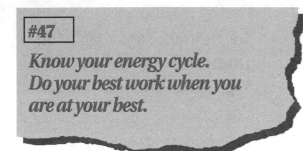

#47

Know your energy cycle. Do your best work when you are at your best.

For instance, you may be an early morning person. If so, schedule your most important activities, as much as possible, during these time periods to achieve greater productivity. (How many of you haven't found your energy cycle yet?)

Of course, you will have to be flexible. If your morning energy cycle runs from 8:00 a.m. to 9:30 a.m., you may plan important work at that time, but your boss or someone else may interrupt you to discuss a crisis that has developed. In that case, you probably wouldn't say: "Sorry, boss. I can't meet with you now. I'm in the middle of my energy cycle."

However, try to maximize your productivity as much as possible by using your energy cycle to your advantage.

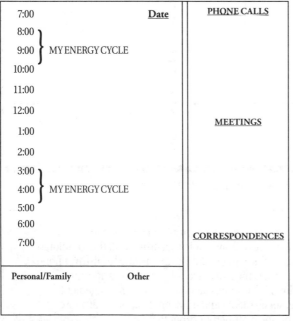

Figure 5: Schedule your most important activities during the hours you are most productive.

#42

Check your progress three times a day to be sure that your behavior matches your plan.

These are your opportunities to ask yourself whether you are accomplishing your plan for the day. On most days, if you are accomplishing at least half to two-thirds of what you set out to do, you will likely experience success in the long run.

But if you find yourself not following through on most days, that is a sign you are probably being consumed by too many mosquitoes—too many interruptions, distractions, meetings, and other low-payoff activities. Discipline yourself to get back on track.

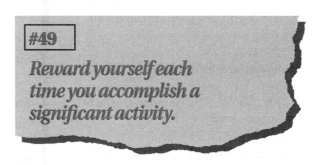

#49

Reward yourself each time you accomplish a significant activity.

It's up to you to determine what is significant. The little rewards you give to yourself are a way of using "positive self-talk," so that you can create a mind-set of self-confidence and high self-esteem. Rewards do not need to be on a grand scale. Little things can mean a lot—a cup of coffee, a special lunch, flowers on your desk, a new self-help book, an audio or video CD/DVD. You decide.

Suggestion: If you are a supervisor, take every opportunity to sincerely recognize and reward the good work of others!

The Process of Achieving Productivity

Here is a summary of the process for achieving greater productivity in your business and personal life. It is based on striving for payoff through productive goal-setting or goal management.

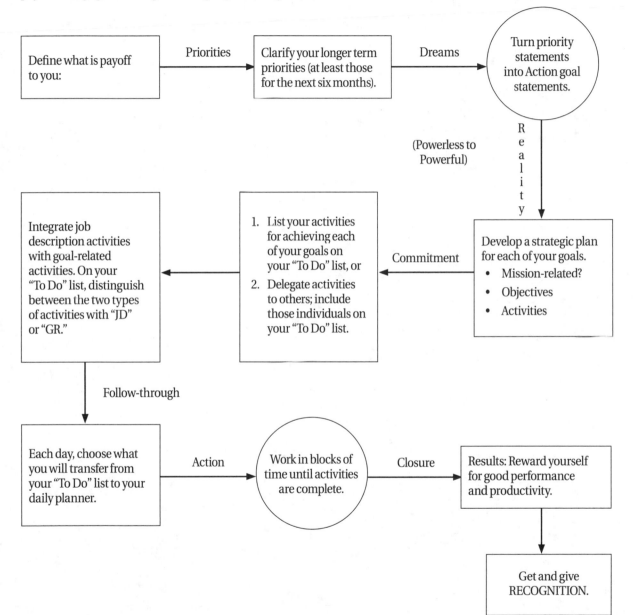

Figure 6: Flowchart of productivity.

CHAPTER 8

How to Be More Productive on Projects

What Is a Project?

Most of this book so far has focused on working on priorities, goals, and activities to achieve greater productivity. This chapter is about working on projects. Project management is a little different.

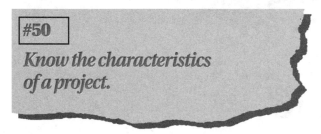

#50

Know the characteristics of a project.

Here are some of them:

There isn't usually a great deal of past experience to draw from. Projects are usually new and unique.

- Projects have a specific deadline and activities within projects have specific deadlines.
- Projects involve a series of "interdependencies." That is, the process of carrying out a project is much like stacking a pile of blocks. The blocks at the top are dependent on the blocks at the bottom.
- There are limited resources. You only have so much time, money, and human resources for carrying out a project
- There is sometimes very limited supervisory control. You can be responsible for overseeing and managing a project although the people who are working on it may actually report to someone else each day.

#51

Use project management tools when working on a specific project.

Many tools are available for helping you make your projects more productive.

Here are five:

- A clearly-stated goal
- A work breakdown structure
- A flow chart
- A budget
- Project management software

> *"Man's greatest experience— the one that brings supreme exultation—is spiritual, not physical. It is the catching of some vision of the universe and translating it into a poem or work of art, into a Sermon on the Mount, into a Gettysburg Address, into a mathematical formula that unlocks the doors of atomic energy."*
>
> William O. Douglas

Projects Need Goals!

#52

Set a clearly stated, action-oriented project goal.

One of the primary reasons projects don't get done is that the goal is never clearly stated. This is a major problem because many times, the people who are working on a project are from various departments and they don't see how they fit in or are aligned with the project. If the goals, activities, and payoff are more clearly defined in their own department, that is where their allegiance will be.

When setting up your project goal, remember the **ACTION** criteria:

Are measurable and reachable

Compatible with your mission

Time-specific

In writing

Ownership (commitment) and accountability

Negotiated (agreed upon)

Example of an action-oriented project goal:
To purchase a new office building by May 15 (year) and to refurbish it for moving in by November 15 (year).

Working on a project is like putting together a jigsaw puzzle:

Where do you start when you put together a jigsaw puzzle? Probably on the corners or borders.
What else do you do?

- Turn the pieces right side up.
- Sort by color, perhaps.
- Divide the labor if more than one person is working on the puzzle: one person works on the upper left border, another on the upper right, and so on.

But what must you do before you ever start to put the puzzle together? Look at the picture on the box. And, what if the box is missing and you have thousands of puzzle pieces scattered about your table? You are likely frustrated and demotivated.

You see the point. For a project to be successful, all the individuals working on it need to see "the picture on the box." Help them to see it by setting a clearly defined goal.

YOU TRY IT!

Exercise 6: Setting Action-oriented Project Goals
List a few of the major projects you need to work on during the next six months:

1. _____

2. _____

3. _____

4. _____

Choose one of the projects you listed and write an action-oriented project goal for it:

_____

_____

_____

_____

_____

_____

_____

_____

_____

_____

_____

_____

_____

_____

_____

Work Breakdown Structures

Many of us grew up learning to think in outline form and by making lists. But outlines and lists don't work for some people who think pictorially. These people are more likely to be productive if they can visualize their tasks and how they fit into the total project.

A Work Breakdown Structure can be a great visual way to break a project down into bite-size pieces. Each of the boxes in the WBS has a name. They are called work packages.

Work Breakdown Structures can be used for personal projects as well as for work-related projects (landscaping your yard, writing a term paper, planning a wedding). The key is in changing the project's perspective from a large, unwieldy project into a series of bite-size activities.

Figure 7 shows a WBS an author could use to write and publish a book.

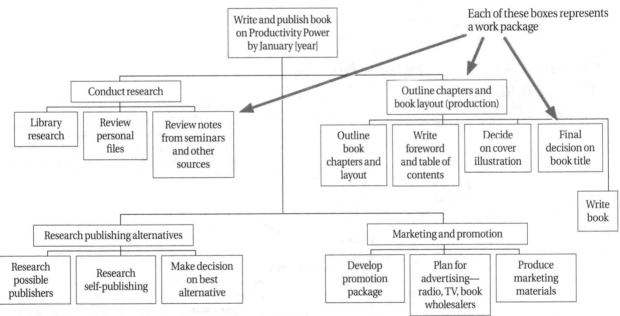

Figure 7: Work Breakdown Structure an author could use to write a book.

If there are people you will be distributing work packages to, give them the big picture. When does their job start and finish? How does it fit into the whole project?

Giving Order to Projects

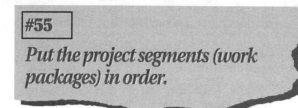

#55

Put the project segments (work packages) in order.

Here are some things to keep in mind as you do so:

1. A project involves a series of interdependencies (activities that are dependent on earlier activities being accomplished). For example, a book can't be written until the research is complete. Marketing materials can't be produced until the book's content is known.

2. One of the best ways to put the work packages in order is to number them.

3. Frequently, more than one work package is accomplished at the same time (simultaneous work packages). You can give each of those simultaneous work packages the same number or use letters to distinguish them (1A and 1B).

4. Estimate the time needed to complete each work package. Be careful to allow enough time to do quality work.

5. Next, you can begin to flow chart the project through another kind of picture called a bar chart or Gantt chart, named after its founder Henry Gantt.

#56

Flowchart your project by using bar charts (Gantt chart).

The dotted lines represent "slack time." In other words, Work Package 7 is scheduled to be accomplished between weeks 6 and 8. However, Work Package 8 can't begin until Week 9. Therefore, whoever is working on Work Package 7 can take one extra week, if necessary.

In Figure 8, the vertical axis shows numbers that correspond with a legend that lists the work packages.

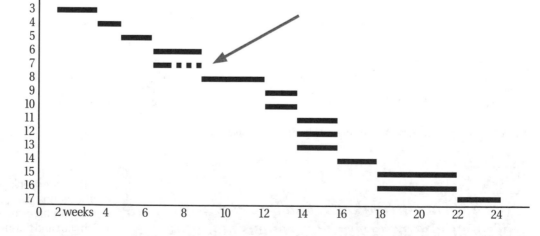

The horizontal axis shows the schedule or time frame for the project as a whole and for each project work package.

Figure 8. Example of bar chart or Gantt chart.

Other Flowcharts

#57

When you have a project involving a number of activities that are happening at the same time, consider using network diagrams.

Network diagrams are derived from two sources:

1. *Program Evaluation Review Technique* (PERT), which the U.S. Navy developed in the late 1950s at the beginning of the aerospace program.

2. *Critical Path Method* (CPM), also developed in the late 1950s, by the DuPont Corporation as a way of sequencing the steps for properly maintaining its facilities to minimize downtime.

The best techniques of each method have been combined into *network diagrams.*

Figure 9 shows a network diagram with three paths of activity. Each activity is represented by a circle (node) with a number in the middle. That number corresponds to a legend that identifies each activity.

In Figure 9, the time frames for each activity are broken down in two-week increments.

The whole project is scheduled to take 14 weeks. Activities #1 – 4 are expected to take two weeks. Activities #1 – 3 are expected to take three weeks.

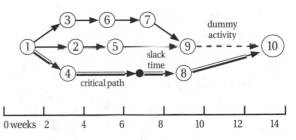

Figure 9. Example of a network diagram.

Here are some additional elements of network diagrams:

- *Critical path.* The longest path through the network. In this example, activities 1, 4, 8, and 10 make up the critical path. A delay on the critical path will delay the whole project. A delay on another path won't. The thick line that runs parallel to the regular lines on the critical path connote the critical path.

- *Slack time.* This means that Activity #4 is scheduled to be completed by Week 6. However, Activity #8 can't begin until week eight. Therefore, those working on Activity #4 have two weeks of slack time to complete their activity, if necessary. But don't encourage people to use slack time unless it is really necessary. Encourage them to stay on schedule.

- *Burst.* Activity #1 must be completed before activities #2 and #3 can begin. Once #1 is completed, the other two can begin at the same rime. Activities #2 and #3 are dependent on Activity #1.

- *Merge (or sink).* Two or more activities must be completed before the next activity can begin. Activity #9 is dependent upon Activities #5 and #7 being accomplished.

- *Dummy activity* or downtime. Represented by the dotted line, "dummy activity" means nothing is happening on a path of activity. All activity on the path ended at the previous point.

Network Diagrams

Some important points about network diagrams:

✓ Network diagrams show interdependencies and simultaneous activities more clearly than bar charts. (However, bar charts are more easily understood.)

✓ Drawing network diagrams is time-consuming and requires practice.

✓ Network diagrams can be most helpful on larger projects involving many activities that are happening at the same time.

✓ Using network diagrams can help you allocate human and other resources more efficiently because you will be able to visualize all the activities throughout the project. You will be prepared for multiple activities that may need multiple resources.

✓ Network diagrams aren't suited for every project. For many of your projects, particularly personal ones or smaller ones, you may choose to use work breakdown structures and bar charts.

#58

Involve your project team in the planning process and let your team help you decide which planning tools to use.

1. Involve others early—right when planning begins.
2. Decide together which tools you will use—work breakdown structures, bar charts, network diagrams, or a combination.
3. Assign project team members to develop these flowcharts.
4. Use computer software, when necessary, to assist in the process.

Using Project Management Software

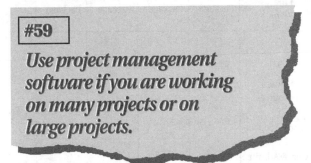

#59

Use project management software if you are working on many projects or on large projects.

What constitutes a large project?

Generally, large projects are those that will last for at least three months and have at least 8 to 10 work packages.

Here's how project management software will help you carry out projects with greater productivity:
Comprehensive packages will help you to draw work breakdown structures, bar charts, and network diagrams. Some packages will help you to estimate the time needed for completing project activities and to budget costs. Also, when there are changes in project scope, you can update your computer models without starting all over again. In other words, you can update your project plans when changes are necessary. Be aware that, generally, project management software is not extremely user friendly. Most comprehensive packages have a somewhat lengthy learning curve and require repeated use for a user to become proficient. However, once you learn it, the software can be a valuable timesaver and an analytical tool.

Budgeting Your Project Costs

#60

Be sure that each project has a specific budget.

One mistake project managers often make is not clarifying the line item budget for each project. Instead, the project leader is asked to spend funds out of the department budget. Here's what usually happens:

1. The project leader and team spend money freely to purchase project resources since there are no budget restraints or parameters.
2. Somewhere along the way, too much money is spent, but the project team claims it wasn't aware of the limits.
3. The project leader and possibly other team members are reprimanded for spending excessively.

If you are a project leader, you are in a no-win situation if you don't have a specific budget.

When you develop a budget, consider the line items that will likely be a part of your project budget.

Line Items	Work Package #1	Work Package #2	Work Package #3	Work Package #4
Human Resources				
Fringe Benefits				
Gen. & Admin.				
Materials				
Supplies				
Postage				
Telephone				
Rent				
Equipment Rental				
Advertising				
Equipment				
Total				

Figure 10. Example of a budget form.

- *Human resources* (also referred to as labor). This line item includes the wages paid to those who are working directly on your project each day. The key word is "directly." They are employees who are thoroughly involved in the project.

- *Fringe benefits* (sometimes called overhead burden). This includes the cost of all benefits for each employee. Benefits are usually figured at between 25 percent to 40 percent per employee. It becomes too cumbersome to figure actual cost per employee. Take an average.

- *General and administrative* (the cost of management and support services). This figure includes support services (data processing, secretarial, hiring, etc.) and outside consulting services (engineering, training, etc.). These are people, either inside or outside the company, who are not involved in the project on a daily basis.

- *Materials* (refers to all material items that go directly into the project). These are the items that become part of the project. For example, lumber and nails become part of a house if your project is to build a house.

- *Supplies* (refers to items that are used in support of the project). These include, pencils, paper, staplers, paper clips, and similar items.

- *Other line items to consider* (postage, telephones, equipment, rent, equipment rental, advertising). The nature of your project will help to determine what other line items you will need. You may need to modify the budget form to include your specific line items. If you budget by work package, each person responsible for the work package is also accountable for a budget.

Holding Project Team Meetings

#62

Hold regular project team meetings to study and analyze the progress of the project.

Here are some reasons why regular project meetings are important:

- To bring project participants together (Many times, because those who are working on projects are from various departments, they don't naturally see each other.)
- To share information and project progress
- To solve project problems and make decisions
- To celebrate successes and deal effectively with failures

#65

Each project meeting should include a discussion of:

- *Time:* Is the project on schedule?
- *Cost:* Is the project within budget?
- *Performance:* Are the work packages being completed and, if so, are they being completed with quality?
- *Problem solving/Decision making:* If there are problems, have they been properly identified and has a process for problem solving/decision making begun?

#64

Project meetings should be set and scheduled before the project begins.

For example, agree to meet every week on Friday between 10:00 a.m. and 11:00 a.m. and decide on a meeting place that is convenient for everyone.

Dimensions of Project Management

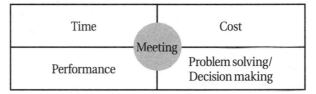

Time	Cost
Performance	Problem solving/ Decision making

(Meeting at center)

Most meetings exist for solving problems and making decisions. If the people in the meeting are immobilized by fear to make a decision, then the project comes to an abrupt halt. (See the Productivity Paradigm in Chapter 1.) If that happens, the delay may throw the project off schedule (or off its critical path), which will waste money, time, and resources and result in lower productivity.

Special considerations for project meetings:

- Always work from an agenda. Be sure it is distributed at least two days before the meeting. (For more about meetings, see Chapter 12.)
- After the meeting, distribute a brief summary (two pages or less) that lists key actions and decisions and who took responsibility for following through on the decisions (this step addresses accountability).
- Be sure the meeting room is properly furnished. Since project management relies on visual tools (WBS, bar charts, network diagrams, etc.), be sure to have proper audiovisual equipment available to display the visuals.

The Process of Achieving Productivity

Here is a summary of the process for achieving greater productivity in your business and personal life by striving for payoff through the process of project management.

A Flow Chart for Project Management Productivity and Success

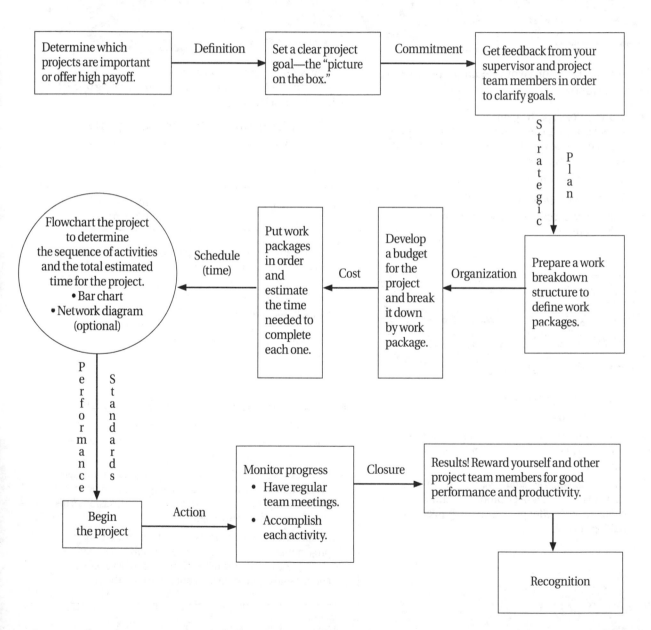

Figure 11. Follow this process for carrying out your projects and you will likely be successful.

The Parallels of Goal Management and Project Management

Although there are differences between goal management and project management, there are also parallels. Here is a comparison of the two processes.

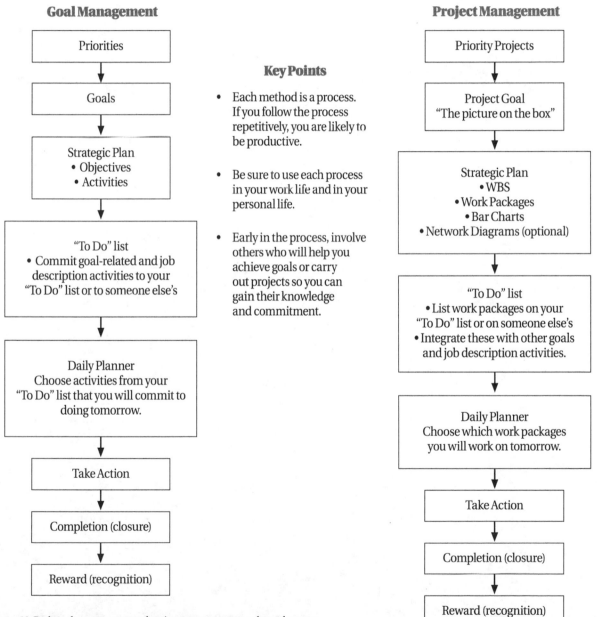

Goal Management

- Priorities
- Goals
- Strategic Plan
  - Objectives
  - Activities
- "To Do" list
  - Commit goal-related and job description activities to your "To Do" list or to someone else's
- Daily Planner
  Choose activities from your "To Do" list that you will commit to doing tomorrow.
- Take Action
- Completion (closure)
- Reward (recognition)

Key Points

- Each method is a process. If you follow the process repetitively, you are likely to be productive.

- Be sure to use each process in your work life and in your personal life.

- Early in the process, involve others who will help you achieve goals or carry out projects so you can gain their knowledge and commitment.

Project Management

- Priority Projects
- Project Goal "The picture on the box"
- Strategic Plan
  - WBS
  - Work Packages
  - Bar Charts
  - Network Diagrams (optional)
- "To Do" list
  - List work packages on your "To Do" list or on someone else's
  - Integrate these with other goals and job description activities.
- Daily Planner
  Choose which work packages you will work on tomorrow.
- Take Action
- Completion (closure)
- Reward (recognition)

Figure 12. Both goal management and project management are dependent on a process that includes setting priorities and goals.

CHAPTER 9

Making Changes for Greater Productivity

> "If you want to make enemies, try to change something."
>
> Woodrow Wilson

That Unholy Obstacle:
The Sacred Cow

There's at least one sacred cow lumbering around in every business. And for every impatient workhorse who wants to get it out of the way, you'll find half a dozen members of the organization feeding the animal on the sly to keep it alive.

A sacred cow is an unwritten rule or hallowed article of business dogma that is jealously defended by people who would rather limp than undergo a minor operation; it is the ultimate veto produced by the opposition when all other forms of argument fail; it is "We've never done it that way before" or " We tried it once and it didn't work" or "The chief is dead set against humour in advertising" or "The union wouldn't stand for it."

Sacred cows cost industry millions of dollars a year simply by obstructing progress. Yet you can get rid of most of them through persistent questioning: "WHY didn't it work before?" "WHEN was it tried?" "WHO tried it?"

In other words, before you can get around a sacred cow, you must WANT to.

Source: Frederick Perves, *Management Review*

■ ■ ■

*"Slaying sacred cows
makes great steaks."*

Dan Nicolosi

The Need for Change

How well do human beings accept change? Not very well.

Following the processes described in this book may require you to approach work differently than you've been used to. Perhaps you'll need to develop some new habits. They may include:

1. Setting you own goals.
2. Defining strategic plans.
3. Learning a new way to use your "To Do" list.
4. Learning to use a day planner.

5. Learning to integrate routine, job description activities with goal-related activities.
6. Involving and working well with others to achieve results together.

#65

Realize that setting goals for your key priorities and projects requires change.

"When you're through changing, you're through."

Bruce Barton

There are three stages of change that can help you deal more effectively with change:

Step 1: Awareness

You become aware that something needs to change. Perhaps as you are reading this book, you are becoming aware of changes that you need to make.

Example: You may look in the mirror and notice that your waistline has grown. At first, you wish and hope that it will go away. However, you find that wishing and hoping won't work. (Powerless)

Step 2: Commitment

You decide to do something about the behavior that needs to change, so you write a specific goal (Action goal). Instead of wishing and hoping, you now have a commitment to change.

Example: To lose that waistline, you set a goal to lose twelve pounds in three months. (Powerful)

Step 3: Discipline

The change in behavior may be (and usually is) more difficult than you thought it would be. In fact, there may be several unforeseen obstacles.

Example: As you try to lose weight, you realize you have to give up some of your favorite foods. Also, the pounds aren't coming off as quickly as you thought they would. You begin to waiver and rationalize: "What's the use? I'll just gain it back anyway."

You could be thinking: "Hey, I know all of this. I know there are changes I need to make to be more productive. I know that setting goals is important to create commitment. I'm aware of how important it is to be disciplined. That's the hard part! Tell me how to be disciplined."

O.K., turn the page. →

How to Be Disciplined

It is important to be aware of what happens to you as you discipline yourself to change.

Discipline ——————————— **Cognitive Dissonance**

What is cognitive dissonance?

Cognitive means "the ability to reason." Dissonance means "out of harmony."
If you put the two terms together, they mean "out of harmony with your own reasoning."

Example: You are trying to lose weight, but it is more difficult than you thought it would be. You begin to waiver.
"Do I really want to lose weight? Yes, because I'll look and feel better and will probably be in better health. But, right now when I'm making the change and passing up these donuts, I don't know if I really want to lose weight that much. Besides, I'll just gain it back."

This internal struggle is called *cognitive dissonance*.

Here is a tip for overcoming cognitive dissonance and staying disciplined:

DREAM of your success.

#66 **D**efine your goals specifically and keep them before you visually.

That way they serve as a reminder of what you are trying to accomplish. (Post your weight loss goal on your refrigerator. Keep a copy of the goal on your bulletin board at work.)

#67 **R**einforce yourself with positive self-talk.

Concentrate on what you can do instead of on what you can't accomplish. ("I know I can lose twelve pounds. It's just four pounds a month" versus "I never stick to these diets, besides who will care whether I lose weight? I'll just regain it.")

#68 **E**ncouragement through a support system of family, friends, co-workers and others.

These are people you can talk to when you're having difficulty with the change.

#69 **A**ttention to what success looks like.

See yourself being successful. (Visualize how you will look if you lose twelve pounds. Keep that picture in your mind.)

#70 **M**ini-reward yourself for your little victories.

Remember, you will use a process for setting goals and for following through on them. The process requires that you break your goals and projects down into bite-size pieces called activities. Each time you accomplish one of these activities, reward yourself.

Discovering Your Own Path for Productivity

The Calf Path

One day through the primeval wood, a calf walked home as good calves should.
But made a trail all bent askew, a crooked trail as all calves do.
Since then three hundred years have fled, and I infer the calf is dead.
But still he left behind his trail, and thereby hangs my moral tale.

The trail was taken up next day, by a lone dog that passed that way;
And then a wise bell-wether sheep pursued the trail o'er vale and steep,
And drew the flock behind him, too, as good bell-wethers always do.
And from that day, o'er hill and glade, through those old woods a path was made.

And many men wound in and out, and dodged and turned and bent about,
And uttered words of righteous wrath, because 'twas such a crooked path;
But still they followed—do not laugh—the first migrations of that calf.

And through this winding wood-way stalked, because he wobbled when he walked.
This forest path became a lane, that bent and turned and turned again;
This crooked lane became a road, where many a poor horse with his load,
Toiled on beneath the burning sun, and traveled some three miles in one.

And thus a century and a half, they trod the footsteps of that calf.
The years passed on in swiftness fleet, the road became a village street;
And this, before men were aware, a city's crowded thoroughfare.
And soon the central street was this, of a renowned metropolis;
And men two centuries and a half, trod in the footsteps of that calf.

Each day a hundred thousand rout, followed this zigzag calf about,
And o'er his crooked journey went, the traffic of a continent.
A hundred thousand men were led, by one calf near three centuries dead.
They followed still his crooked way, and lost one hundred years a day;
For thus such reverence is lent, to well-established precedent.

A moral lesson this might teach, were I ordained and called to preach;
For men are prone to go it blind, along the calf-paths of the mind,
And work away from sun to sun, to do what other men have done.
They follow in the beaten track, and out and in, and forth and back,
And still their devious course pursue, to keep the path that others do.

They keep the path a sacred groove, along which all their lives they move;
But how the wise old wood-gods laugh, who saw the first primeval calf.
Ah, many things this tale might teach—but I am not ordained to preach.

Sam Walter Foss

Removing Obstacles

Now you know about the processes for goal management, project management, and handling change. But isn't it true that there will be obstacles that will keep you from accomplishing your daily plan?

Yes. Here are some of the major ones:

Interruptions —————————

> You arrive at work with your daily plan, but almost immediately people start interrupting you with questions, comments about the great game that was on television last night, and other chit-chat.

Telephone —————————

> It won't stop ringing. Just as you are really concentrating on an activity, the phone jolts you back to reality. It calls out for you to answer it. Or, you waste time trying to reach someone else in an endless game of phone tag.

Meetings —————————

> You begin to feel like your whole working life revolves around meetings. As you sit there listening to the person next to you expound and pontificate, you think, "What am I doing here?"

Too much paperwork and lack of organization —————————

> "I know it's here somewhere" is the battle cry. Just when you get your desk cleared off and organized, others start "dumping" on you again. You work extra hours just to keep up with the reports, minutes, and periodicals that are a part of your job. The faster you go, the "behinder" you get.

> *"Obstacles are those frightful things you see when you take your eyes off your goal."*
>
> Hannah More

Procrastination

Your motto becomes: "Wait until tomorrow. You'll see. I'll get it done then." Tomorrow becomes an endless string of days with good intentions but poor performance. You feel like you have so much work that something has to give. You tackle the things that are most immediate, hoping for more time tomorrow. Unfortunately, each day has but twenty-four hours.

Your boss

You arrive at work with your plan and sit down to tackle it. Your supervisor comes up to you and says: "We have an emergency in the field. We need to talk." Or, you are in the middle of an important project and the supervisor rushes up to you with yet another new project that must be finished immediately. You think, "Doesn't this person know that I'm already overloaded?"

Do these obstacles sound familiar? They probably do. They were culled from an informal survey of seminar participants who were asked, "What are the obstacles that keep you from accomplishing your daily plan?"

As Dr. Abraham Maslow said, "If the only tool in your toolbox is a hammer, the whole world begins to look like a nail." In other words, if you don't develop new tools to deal with a changing environment, the environment will always have control over you.

You can either let obstacles control you, or you can learn how to take control of the obstacles by using the tools at your disposal. Much of the remainder of this book will give you tools for dealing effectively with these obstacles.

"Preconceived notions are the locks on the door to wisdom."

Merry Brown

CHAPTER 10

How to Handle Interruptions

> "We have met the enemy, and they is us."
>
> Pogo (cartoon character)

Dealing With the Most Persistent Interruptions

#72

Learn how to say no through the USA method.

Scenario: You are sitting at your desk getting ready to begin an activity that you've slotted to do from 10:00 a.m. until 11:00 a.m. But a co-worker walks up to your desk and says: "Could I talk with you for a few minutes? I'm having a real problem with the second step of the development project, and I'd really appreciate your advice."

What do you want to say to this person?
What you might be thinking is "No, go away. I'll talk with you later. Can't you see I'm busy? Leave me alone. Get lost." And so on.

You aren't likely to say any of those things because it would be rude or impolite. To the other person, this "problem" may be a major concern that could affect you too. If the person interrupting you is a co-worker or someone you supervise, you should want to help, but now may not be the best time. The problem may be important, but it probably isn't something that must be resolved immediately.

But what if the person who's interrupting is your supervisor? You might feel that you must drop everything for your supervisor.

There is a simple method for handling these abrupt interruptions: It's called the USA method of saying no.

The method requires practice. As you use it, you'll be amazed at how well you'll begin controlling interruptions rather than allowing them to control you.

UNDERSTANDING STATEMENT OR STATEMENT OF EMPATHY.

Example: "Bob, I'm sure this problem (or concern) is important." (It is to Bob and it may be to you too. But it probably isn't urgent.)

SITUATION STATEMENT.

You make a statement that explains the present situation.

Example: "I'm working on a report that I promised myself I would finish by 11:00 a.m."

ACTION STATEMENT.

You make a statement that describes what you will do.

Example: "Let's get together this afternoon between 2:00 and 2:15. I'll meet you at your desk (or in the conference room.)"

Pay particular attention to how these examples allow you to control the environment. *You* set the appointment time and *you* suggest meeting at Bob's desk or in the conference room rather than at your own desk. This gives you the freedom to escape if the meeting goes on too long.

"*If you never say no, what is your yes worth?*"

#73

Go to the other person's desk or office or meet in the conference room or other neutral place. Meeting outside your office allows you to control the environment. You can wrap up the meeting and leave.

Learning to Say No

What if Bob says: "Gosh, I can't meet with you at 2:00. I'll be in another meeting. Also, I think our meeting will take longer than fifteen minutes."

How would you respond? _____

_____

_____

Suggested response:

"All right. Then how about if we meet between 3:30 and 4:00?"

Don't say: "Well, when is a good time for you and how long do you think our meeting will take?"

If you give the second response, you are no longer in control of the conversation or the negotiating. You have inadvertently transferred the control to the other person—not a good idea.

> | #74 |
>
> *Maintain control of interruptions by controlling the conversation and negotiation. <u>Pre-state</u> the conditions of the meeting.*

(In effect, you are saying "I will meet with you under these pre-stated conditions.")

How do you use the USA method to handle interruptions from your supervisor?

The supervisor calls you into his or her office for a conference: "Ann, I hate to interrupt you, but we have a real problem in the field. I need to talk with you right away. Could I see you in my office?"

Use the USA method to handle the interruption:

U NDERSTANDING STATEMENT. "I'm sure this is an important problem."

S ITUATION STATEMENT. "I'm working on that report you requested by noon."

A CTION STATEMENT. "Would you like me to defer the report until later this afternoon so I can meet with you now?"

By stating the situation, you are helping your supervisor see your perspective. Sometimes a supervisor is concentrating on his or her perspective until you paint a picture.

You have just transferred the responsibility for action, in this case, making a decision, to your supervisor. In fact, you are saying: "Do you know that there is something else you wanted me to do that is also important? I can't meet *and* finish the report." However, you are saying it in a way that your supervisor can accept.

When is an interruption not really an interruption?

Answer: When it is a regular part of your job.

Example: If you work in Customer Service, your job may be to handle phone calls all day or to field customer concerns. Your regular job activities should not be misconstrued as interruptions.

Handling the Professional Interrupter

The USA method will work about 80 percent of the time. (Remember the 80-20 rule?) But what about the persistent 20 percent who don't take the hint? These people are professional interrupters. They make a career out of interrupting others.

Everyone knows these kinds of people. They start talking and won't stop. They continue for about 15 minutes. When they finally pause, you still don't know what they said or why they are bothering you.

Here's how to handle professional interrupters:

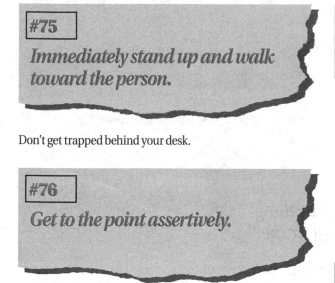

#75

Immediately stand up and walk toward the person.

Don't get trapped behind your desk.

#76

Get to the point assertively.

What do we need to talk about? How can I help you? What do we need to discuss today?

Example: "No, I missed the game last night, Tom. What do we need to discuss? I'm real busy on the Acme Project right now."

The professional interrupter usually doesn't respond to your question. He or she just keeps talking.

#77

Repeat your statement.

This is called "the broken record technique."

Example: "Tom, what do we need to talk about? I'm real busy on the Acme Project right now."

It's necessary to repeat the message until the other person receives it.

It is important to use this technique with professional interrupters because they are poor listeners. They are too busy talking.

#78

If you determine that the interruption is unwarranted, walk away from the person and your desk, but maintain eye contact with the person so you don't appear rude.

What is the professional interrupter likely to do? Follow you. This is called postural echo or mirroring. The other person does what you do. When you are far enough away from your desk, say to the other person assertively, "I must really get back to what I was doing." Then walk away, back to your desk.

When They Still Don't Get the Hint

What about those few people who still don't get the hint—who follow you back to your desk, continuing to talk "at" you?

There's no easy (diplomatic) way to handle these people.

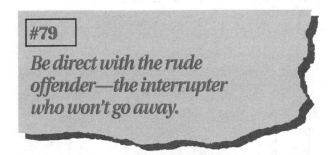

#79

Be direct with the rude offender—the interrupter who won't go away.

Say, "I really can't tolerate any more interruptions." Realize, though, that the other person may be offended or have hurt feelings. You have to look at your alternatives and decide the best way to deal with the problem—to let it continue or to deal with it now.

Some other ways to deal with interruptions:

#80

Maintain your work posture. If someone approaches you to interrupt, continue what you are doing—reading the mail, punching in the numbers on the telephone, dictating, and so forth.

Usually, the other person will get the hint and say, "Oh, I see you're busy right now." That gives you the opportunity to gracefully decline the interruption.

#81

Stand up to talk.

If you are interrupted or if you must interrupt someone else, try to hold your informal meeting or discussion standing up rather than seated. Your body posture will communicate a sense of urgency.

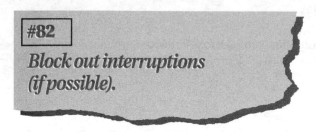

#82

Block out interruptions (if possible).

The way your desk is situated could be inviting interruptions. Does it face a hallway? Is it right out in the open? Is it positioned in a way that allows you to frequently make eye contact with others?

Is it convenient for others to interrupt you? Can they sit on the edge of your desk or in the chair that is next to your desk?

If so, try rearranging your desk and office.

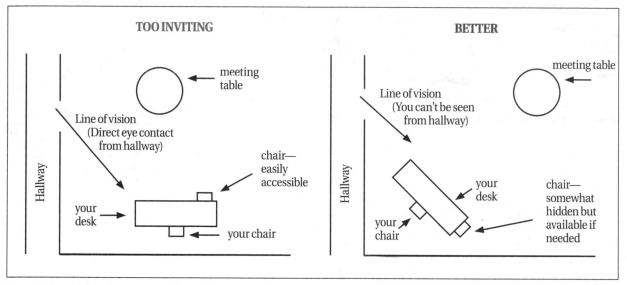

Figure 13. Suggested way to arrange an office to discourage interruptions.

Obviously, it may be impractical to reposition yourself totally. You may have a built-in desk, or you may be limited by phone lines, computer lines, and wall outlets. The diagrams in Figure 13 are meant to enlighten you about the possibilities.

Handling Interruptions if You Are a Supervisor

If you supervise others and you are frequently interrupted, it might be a sign that you aren't spending enough time during the day with those you supervise.

#83

*Practice Management
By Walking Around (MBWA).*

Here's how it works:

✓ Pick out 45 minutes to one hour each day (that you are in the office) to practice management by walking around, but *with* purpose.

✓ Indicate that time block on your day planner.

✓ Be specific about who you plan to meet with. Perhaps there are two or three individuals you need to question about the activities or projects they are working on.

✓ Schedule appointments with those individuals first thing in the morning. Don't just interrupt them. Set the tone for your "meeting" with them by pre-stating the conditions: "Steve, could we get together for about 10 minutes between 9:20 and 9:30 this morning? I'll come over to your desk."

✓ Be prepared to meet each person with a handwritten agenda. Then get right to the point.

✓ Be sure to discuss the other person's concerns and to answer their questions.

✓ Summarize the discussion.

Residual effect: As you walk to your meetings, others you supervise will probably see you and may ask to speak with you. Because you have built in the time on your day planner, you probably can have a mini-discussion right on the spot. This process will cut down on your interruptions and help you direct the work of others. Try it.

Keep a "discussion file" for each person you supervise. Drop into it the notes and questions you want to ask of your staff members. Then when you practice Management By Walking Around, you can ask all your questions and make your comments. By using this approach, you'll avoid frequently interrupting your staff.

Steve	9:20-9:30
1. Check on deadline date for building project.	
2. Answer his question about extended leave.	
3. See if he paid in-service from Smith Company.	
4. Check on January 15 training meeting.	

Figure 14. Sample agenda for meeting with employees while practicing Management By Walking Around.

Dealing With Interruptions at Home

Certainly, many of the ways for handling interruptions at work also apply at home. Here are a few extra thoughts about dealing with interruptions at home:

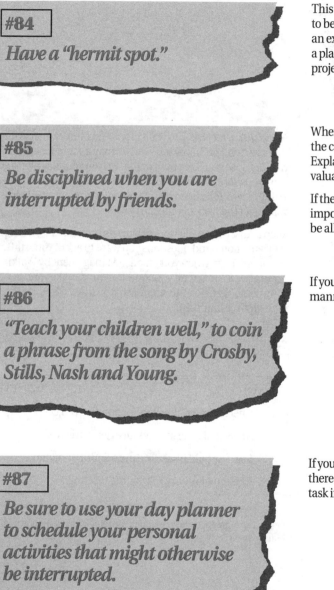

#84

Have a "hermit spot."

This is a place in your home or apartment where you can go to be alone. It may be a den, a sewing room, a potting shed, an extra bedroom, a workshop, or someplace similar. It is a place where you can be alone to work on special home projects and activities.

#85

Be disciplined when you are interrupted by friends.

When friends and neighbors interrupt your tasks (washing the car, finishing the laundry, cutting the grass), stay on task. Explain that you will talk later. This may be one of the most valuable pieces of advice you receive.

If they're really your friends, they'll understand. It is important to have friends, but these relationships should not be all-consuming.

#86

"Teach your children well," to coin a phrase from the song by Crosby, Stills, Nash and Young.

If you have children, teach them early on the value of good manners and of not blatantly interrupting others.

#87

Be sure to use your day planner to schedule your personal activities that might otherwise be interrupted.

If you designate a specific block of time to complete a job, there is a greater chance that you will follow through on the task if interrupted.

CHAPTER 11

Taking Control of the Telephone

"Aren't you glad the telephone wasn't invented by Alexander Graham Siren?"

George Carlin

Using Your Telephone Time Productively

The telephone paradox: If you control the telephone, it can be one of your greatest timesavers. If it controls you, it can become one of your more significant timewasters. You can enhance your control over the telephone by using your daily planner effectively.

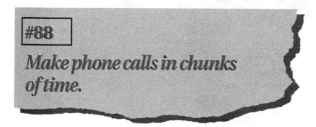

#88

Make phone calls in chunks of time.

Discipline yourself not to be making or answering calls all day long (unless that is the essence of your job—customer service, trouble-shooting, etc.)

7:00		**PHONE CALLS**
8:00	Phone calls to East Coast clients: Tom Harvey, Steve Phillips, Jean Thompson, Gregg Lunt; calls to potential clients	Tom H.
9:00		1. Review brochure 2. Discuss costs 3. Answer questions
10:00		Steve P.
11:00	Staff meeting 10:00-11:30 – Work on proposal for capital funding	1. Review grant proposal
12:00		Jean T.
1:00		1. Set meeting date 2. Review agenda 3. Clarify directions
2:00		Gregg L.
3:00		1. Try to close on order 2. Answer questions
4:00	Phone calls – Mary Anderson, Darla Redner; return calls	
5:00	4:30-5:30 – Review building site plan with project manager	**MEETINGS**

7:00		10:00-11:00
		  Staff meeting
		4:30-5:30
		  Building meeting

Personal/Family	**Other**
• Stop at grocery store for milk on way home • Pick up pictures at lunch break	• Open mail

CORRESPONDENCES
1. Answer general inquiry letters
2. Confirm letter to Barbara Lund

Figure 15. Choose chunks of time in the morning and in the afternoon for scheduling phone calls.

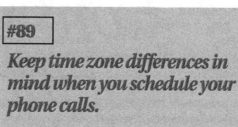

#89

Keep time zone differences in mind when you schedule your phone calls.

If you live in the West, be sure to schedule East Coast calls early. If you live in the East, you obviously will want to schedule your West Coast calls for late morning or early afternoon.

#90

Treat phone calls as meetings.

Always work from a handwritten agenda (See Idea #38 in Chapter 7.) You will appear more self-confident and purposeful to the person you are calling. And because the agenda will keep you from forgetting key points, the time you spend on the telephone will likely be more productive.

Be Prepared When You Make Your Calls

#91

Set the tone for your phone conversations.

Have you ever noticed how much time you can waste talking about the weather, your family, a television program, business rumors, or other nonessential information? Niceties can be important in setting a friendly tone, but be conscious of keeping them to a minimum. Here are some examples of how you can set the tone of your phone conversations.

If you are calling someone:
- "Let me tell you why I called."
- "The reason I'm calling you is . . ."
- "Here's what I'd like to discuss with you . . ."
- "The purpose of my call is . . ."

If someone is calling you:
- "I'm glad you called. How can I help you?"
- "What do we need to discuss today?"
- "Tell me why you called."
- "What can I do for you?"

Be sure to use an upbeat tone of voice.

These salutations may seem simplistic, but sometimes people forget to use them or ignore them altogether. Practice using them to bring your phone conversations to the point.

#92

Use a card file, Rolodex™, or contact list to locate frequently called numbers.

People frequently lose phone numbers and waste a lot of time trying to retrieve those numbers. Here are some ways to organize your important phone numbers.

1. Use a card file or Rolodex™. These contain several cards you can use for writing down telephone numbers and other key information about people or companies you frequently call. Use a separate card for each person or organization.

   You can also staple your business cards to the cards in your Rolodex™. (You may have to cut the business card down to fit the Rolodex™ file card.)

   Write miscellaneous information about the individual or the company on the back of the Rolodex™ card. For example, jot down the best time of day to reach the person and the person's title, characteristics, e-mail address, and other similar information.

2. Store your frequently called numbers in your computer databases and mobile phone contact lists. If you change electronic entries, be sure to update your physical phone list, if applicable.

3. Most day planning systems come with a phone file system. You may choose to use it as your primary telephone reference file, particularly if you travel a great deal and you carry your day planner with you.

"People who get ahead are those who prove they can get things done."

David Kearns

How to Screen Calls

Today's telephone technology opens up all kinds of possibilities for effectively screening calls, but caution and good common sense are still encouraged so that you won't inadvertently lose your clients and colleagues.

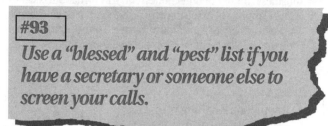

#93

Use a "blessed" and "pest" list if you have a secretary or someone else to screen your calls.

On the surface, this idea may sound arrogant, but if you want to control telephone interruptions, you and the person who screens your calls must determine which calls get through and which do not. Who's blessed and who's a pest?

Have a 5- to 10-minute meeting with your screener/secretary first thing every morning to discuss who you are expecting calls from. Also be sure to list anyone else whose calls should be put through to you.

Remember, make your calls in chunks of time. Follow this principle when you return the calls of those who tried to reach you earlier but whose calls were not routed to you immediately.

#94

Consider your options for screening calls.

Here are some ways to screen calls. The list provides alternatives even for those who run a one-person office.

1. **Voice mail.** If you are a one-person operation or if you work in an office with few employees, voice mail can help you take calls that you can return later. If you use voice mail, update the message to explain why you can't take the calls.

Example: "I will be out of the office from 10:00 a.m. until noon today. Please leave your name, number and a brief message. I'll be pleased to call you back."

Word of caution: Telling callers that you are away applies to offices—and only to those operated by more than one person. If you leave this message on your home phone, you are, in effect, saying this: "Since I'll be gone between 10:00 a.m. and noon, that would be a good time for you to rob me."

- Keep your message brief and to the point. Long-winded messages bore callers. They may hang up before listening to your complete message.

- Speak in an upbeat voice. Some people sound like robots on their messages. Convey enthusiasm. Let your callers know you are pleased they called.

- Be aware of your tone of voice. This goes right along with speaking in an upbeat voice. Record your message in just a little lower tone (not so it's obvious, though). This gives your voice resonance.

Remember that many people do not like to talk to a machine. Make your message as personable and as warm as possible so that the caller will be more likely to leave a message.

2. Answering service. Some people are still annoyed by or hesitant to leave messages on voice mail. An answering service is another alternative for screening calls, particularly if your business is small.

Some of the points in favor of an answering service:

- There is a real person on the line.
- It may make your business appear larger to your customers (if that's the impression you're trying to create).
- Since there is a live person taking the message, the caller may feel freer to leave more information.
- If you have a well-run answering service, the operator can create a very positive impression for your company.

Be careful when you select an answering service.

As with most companies, there are good ones and bad ones. Choose one that:

- Concentrates on good customer service.
- Does a thorough job of training its operators.
- Has very definite procedures for handling calls.
- Hires operators who are committed to performing quality work and who don't consider what they do to be "just a job."
- Above all, talk to the owner or manager. Get an idea of how the company is managed. Determine whether the company really cares about serving you.

"Problems are not stop signs; they are guidelines."

Dr. Robert Schuller

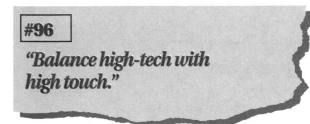

#95

Explore high-tech devices to help you use the telephone more efficiently and to help you be in control.

Always be looking for new time-saving, efficient telephone devices and equipment that can help you be more productive. You already know about some of these, but here's a list to jog your memory:

- Call waiting
- Call forwarding
- Voice mail
- Fax machines (What a great device! Remember, some people learn visually. Fax pictures of your products and services to them.)
- Special headsets that leave your hands free (The good ones also block out background noise.)
- Cell phones (If you happen to be following someone who is talking on theirs in their car, you may not be sure whether having a cell phone is a blessing or a curse. But they can be helpful. Consider a hands-free device for obvious reasons.)
- Smartphones (With all the apps available, you can take your office with you wherever you go.)

#96

"Balance high-tech with high touch."

That was the recommendation of Ron Zemke and Karl Albrecht in their book *Service America* (Dow Jones-Irwin, 1985). Their point: People get frustrated talking to machines. If you sense this is the case with one of your callers, be extra kind and helpful.

Example: "It sounds like you had a difficult time reaching me. I'm pleased that we are able to talk to each other. Let me give you my extension so that next time you call, it will be easier to reach me or my voice mail. Now, how may I help you?"

What to Do to Keep From Being Screened Out

Do you sometimes feel that you are given the third degree when you phone others? Here is what you can do to get through more often to the party you are calling.

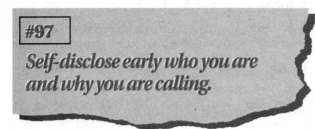

#97

Self-disclose early who you are and why you are calling.

In other words, disarm the screener by disclosing information about yourself and the nature of the call. Speak fairly rapidly and keep your message as brief as possible but still convey important information.

> *Example:* "This is John Reynolds calling from John Reynolds and Associates for Bill Stevens. He attended a seminar I presented last week and he was interested in holding an in-house seminar for your company. I'm calling him to determine his interest. May I speak with Bill, please?"

Note how the caller in the example briefly disclosed a lot of information so that the screener would not have to qualify him. If the caller had just asked, "May I speak with Bill Stevens?" he probably would have heard the usual round of questions:

1. "May I ask who's calling?"
2. "May I tell Bill the nature of the call?"
3. "Is he expecting your call?"
4. "I'm not sure Bill is here. Would you hold while I check?" (Then the screener says to Bill, "Do you know a John Reynolds?")

You can see what happens if you don't self-disclose. Reminder: Be sure to keep the tone of your voice pleasant and upbeat as you self-disclose your message. Also, speak with some sense of urgency since the screener may be a receptionist who is handling the switchboard.

If you follow these suggestions, there is a much greater chance that you will get through to the person you called.

> *"Just because the message may never be received does not mean it is not worth sending."*
>
> Segaki (Japanese Philosopher)

Controlling the Callback

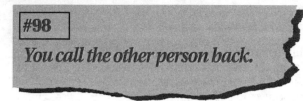

#98

You call the other person back.

You've been trying all morning to reach a client on the opposite coast. Late in the morning, you walk down the hall to get a cup of coffee.

You can guess what happens. Your hard-to-reach client calls you back and you miss the call.

Does this sound like a familiar situation? It has probably happened to all of us. But there is a way to minimize this scenario.

For your most important calls, rather than leave a message for the other person to call you back, set a "phone appointment" to call the person back at a designated time. That way you maintain control of the callback situation.

Example: When you call Mary, the screener says: "Mary is in a meeting right now. Can I take your name and number and have her call you back?"

Gracefully decline, because (1) you will transfer control to Mary, who will call you at her convenience or not at all, or (2) when she calls back, you may well be somewhere else—away from your desk and phone tag begins.

Here's how to gracefully decline transferring control:

Screener: "May I take your name and number and have Mary return your call?"

You: "Could you please tell me when Mary will be available?"

Screener: "I'm not sure, but I know she'll be in a meeting for the rest of the morning."

You: "OK. Would you leave a message for Mary that I will call her again this afternoon at 3:00?"

Screener: "I don't know whether she'll be available."

You: "I'd appreciate it if you would give her the message. I'll try to reach her at 3:00 p.m."

Then, be sure to call back right at 3:00 p.m.

What you have done is set a phone meeting with Mary, even though she hasn't agreed to it. The power of suggestion is such that Mary will be available. Try this technique. It works!

Note: Do this with your most important calls. Use common sense. Sometimes you may feel it is preferable to leave your name and phone number.

Avoiding Phone Tag

Do you spend too much time playing phone tag?

If your answer is a resounding yes, you aren't alone. The cost in lost productivity from phone tag is staggering. According to a survey by Accountemps, we spend 15 minutes a day or 60 hours a year on hold.

In his book *Phone Power How to Make the Telephone Your Most Profitable Business Tool* (G.P. Putnam's Sons, 1986), George Walther notes that the average executive wastes five to seven hours a week playing phone tag.

Here are some tips for minimizing phone tag:

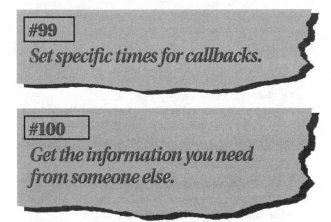

#99

Set specific times for callbacks.

Example: "I'll call Bob again at 2:15 p.m."

Or, if you will be away from your desk, explain that the person you called should call you back between 2:00 p.m. and 3:00 p.m.—if you choose to have that person call you back.

#100

Get the information you need from someone else.

Maybe you don't need to talk to the person you called. Get the information you need from an assistant or secretary. In the majority of cases, you can get the information you need from someone other than the person you called.

#101

Be clear about what you want and when you need it, and clarify who will provide it.

Prepare for the call before you make it to determine specifically why you are making the call. After the conversation, use feedback to verify the facts and what you and the other person agreed to do.

#102

If you will be away from your desk, always let someone know how to reach you.

Much time is wasted playing phone tag because people get "lost" in their own buildings or offices. That is, people step away for a few minutes to get coffee, to meet with another person, to go to the restroom, to use the copy machine, or to take care of some other task. If you let a co-worker or secretary know where you are, that person can immediately let you know when a call is waiting, particularly if it is one that you are expecting.

Taking Phone Messages

#103

Devise a phone message form that will give you accurate information about the caller.

Another productivity killer is incomplete or inaccurate phone messages.

Scenario: You arrive at your office after an appointment. Awaiting you are several of those little pink telephone message forms that say "While You Were Out ..."

You begin making your callbacks. The first person you call greets you with a barrage of hostility—whoa! You weren't expecting it. But you had no warning. You were blind-sided. The message you received included no "past history." Consider using the form in Figure 16 or a variation of it to take phone messages for people in your company.

TELEPHONE MESSAGE

To: _____ Date: _____

From: _____ Time: _____

Company: _____ Phone No.: _____

Person who took message: _____

Purpose of call: _____

_____

Demeanor of caller: _____

Suggestions: _____

_____

Figure 16. Form for taking accurate phone messages.

- **"From"**
  If necessary, ask the message taker to spell the person's name phonetically as well as properly, so that you correctly pronounce the person's name when you return the call.

- **"Purpose of call"**
  A brief statement about why the person called so that you can prepare for the callback.

- **"Demeanor of caller"**
  How did the person calling act? Emotionally upset? Pleasant? Excited? Outgoing?

- **"Suggestions"**
  Ask the message taker to write down any suggestions that would benefit you when you make the callback.

If you are having a problem with someone not returning your calls, try Idea #104 if the person has a fax machine.

#104

On your copier, enlarge the telephone message form in Figure 16, write your message, and fax the completed message to the person you are trying to reach.

If you want to get the other person's attention, make your message stand out from the crowd of other messages.

Remember: E-mail and/or voice mail should remain integral tools for business messaging.

More Excellent Tips for Using the Telephone Efficiently

#105

Eliminate clutter from your desk when you are making or receiving phone calls.

Yes, this is a tough one. Here's what happens. You make a call that requires certain files to be on your desk. You no sooner hang up and someone else calls. You take out new files or other information and place it on top of the files you used before. Before you know it, your desk is cluttered to the point that you can't find what you need, and you are unable to respond efficiently to your caller's questions. You find yourself using these phrases: "I know it's here somewhere. Let me call you back as soon as I find it. It must have disappeared."

Two things have just happened:

1. You have lost productivity.
2. You created an impression in the caller's mind that says "She doesn't have her act together."

> Discipline yourself to clear your desk of the information you used for earlier calls. Focus your attention on the present call.

#106

Stand up to talk.

It is a good idea to stand up during telephone conversations. Here are some reasons why:

✓ It gives you a greater awareness of the time you are on the phone.

✓ Some people seem to think better on their feet.

✓ You can move around freely. You can increase your mobility if you use a long telephone cord. With a long cord, you can more efficiently put your hands on information that you need. When you are standing, you can breathe more efficiently from the diaphragm; therefore, your voice is likely to have greater resonance and projection.

Here's another way that standing up to talk can help you increase your productivity. Use a separate desk that is built into the wall at a slight angle—or a drafting table—to keep your phone and some note paper on. Put a bulletin board above the desk, and keep notes and other information you use frequently posted there. Don't keep a chair next to the desk. If you are in an office that would accommodate a desk of this type, give the idea a try. You'll be surprised at how much your productivity increases.

#107

Take notes during your conversation and write down questions as they occur to you.

Sometimes what the other person says triggers a question, but by the time that person finishes speaking, you may forget your question, which means another phone call later when you remember the question.

CHAPTER 12

Taking Control of Meetings

> "A manager spending more than 25 percent of time in meetings is a sign of malorganization."
>
> Peter Drucker

How to Take Control of Meetings

One high-ranking executive keeps a sign on his desk that says, "Will this meeting bring me closer to my goals?" It reminds him to think before automatically committing to all meetings.

He said that he used to routinely attend meetings when he was asked. He found that often he didn't need to be there. In fact, he said, many times no one needed to be there.

This is not to say that all meetings are unproductive or worthless (just the majority of them). The idea is to be proactive instead of reactive.

If you have no choice and must attend meetings that others call, set an example. Be well prepared.

To find out whether you're attending meetings that you don't need to attend, answer the questions in Exercise 7.

YOU TRY IT!

Exercise 7: Are You in Control of the Meetings You Attend?

Answer these questions:

1. Do you spend too much time in meetings?
   Yes ☐   No ☐

2. Do you attend meetings but don't know why you're there?
   Yes ☐   No ☐

3. Do you attend meetings that last longer than they should?
   Yes ☐   No ☐

4. Do you attend meetings dominated by one or two people?
   Yes ☐   No ☐

Chances are you answered yes to the questions in Exercise 7. How can you take control of meetings even when you're not the meeting planner?

By setting an example to be prepared and to the point. The next several tips reveal some of the specific things you can do to take control of meetings.

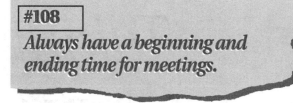

#108

Always have a beginning and ending time for meetings.

Here's the way it usually goes when a meeting is being arranged: "How about if we get together Friday at 10:00 a.m.?"

How do you know when this meeting will end? You don't. Here's what you can do to set well-defined time frames for meetings:

- *If you are the meeting planner:* "Let's get together on Friday between 10:00 a.m. and 11:00 a.m. (You have just pre-stated the time conditions you will meet under. See Idea #74 in Chapter 10.)

- *If you have been asked to attend someone's meeting:* "It would help me to know what time the meeting is scheduled to end so I can plan the rest of my day." (By using this phrase, you are helping the other person be more specific about the meeting's time frame.)

- *If the meeting goes on past the assigned ending time:* Be assertive and say, "I would appreciate it if we could begin summarizing the meeting so that we can bring it to a close." (This may be difficult to do, but it is necessary to say to those who continually ignore deadlines, including your boss. Speak up, using a positive, nonthreatening, nonsarcastic tone.)

Preparing Efficiently for Meetings

#109

Circulate an agenda at least two days before the meeting (preferably a week in advance) along with all attachments meeting attendees must study and be prepared to discuss.

#110

If meeting attendees are flying or driving to your meetings, provide them with background information in advance so they can be prepared for the meeting.

This is a must! Idea #118 discusses how the agenda should look, using an extended agenda.

You could be thinking: "What's the use of sending attachments before the meeting? Many of the meeting participants won't read them anyway."

You may be right. But you have at least given participants the opportunity to be prepared. You have transferred responsibility to them. The conscientious people (most of them) will appreciate it.

Listening to an audio file or looking over materials sent by PDF is an easy way for attendees to assimilate information, and it gives them something to do with their downtime while traveling to the meeting.

#111

Once you have defined the time parameters, be sure the meeting starts and ends on time.

Start on time, even if some attendees aren't there. Reward, don't penalize, those who show up on time.

"Show me a person who likes to go to meetings and I'll show you a person who doesn't have enough to do."

Joe Griffith

#112

Always state the meeting's purpose (or primary purpose if there is more than one) at the beginning of the meeting.

By stating the main reason for holding the meeting, everyone is likely to be clear about why you are meeting and why they are there. Write the primary purpose on the agenda. (See Idea #119.)

#113

Summarize meeting decisions.

Summarize throughout the meeting so that everyone is clear about follow-up and follow-through. Meeting participants will then know their role in implementing decisions.

"Committees of ten act now and then. But most jobs are done by committees of one."

C. Northcote Parkinson
(of Parkinson's Law fame)

#114

Begin to summarize the meeting about 10 to 15 minutes before the designated ending time.

Let everyone know that it is nearing the time for the meeting to conclude. Start using words that convey the sense of urgency:

- "Let's begin to list the key points as we get ready to conclude."
- "Let's summarize our decisions and intended actions."
- "As we begin to wrap up this meeting, let's note some of the key points."

#115

Discipline chronic latecomers.

Don't let meeting participants continually get away with being late. Call them aside after the meeting (if you are their supervisor) to directly express your disapproval. Be sure to discipline these employees privately, not in front of the group. If you are not their supervisor, briefly tell your boss that it is unfair and disruptive for people to repeatedly show up late. Be careful to use tact, but do express your displeasure.

Running Efficient Meetings

Make meetings fun, interesting, and exciting.

#116

Try different approaches to encourage people to be on time for meetings.

#117

Assign specific roles to some of your meeting attendees so that they can help make the meetings more productive.

Here are some of them:

- Be sure that every meeting participant has an agenda before the meeting and that it clearly states the meeting's primary purpose and starting and ending time.

- Start with an interesting fact, training video, or something else likely to interest attendees.

- Ask all latecomers to contribute a nickel (or some amount you determine together) for every minute they are late. Give the funds to charity, purchase meeting equipment, or use them for some other worthy cause after the "pot" has built up over a year.

- Have interesting guest speakers from time to time. Be sure they are people who really have something to say and can say it with interest and enthusiasm. Don't invite outside speakers just to fill time. It is a waste of time and money.

- Be sure to ask each meeting participant before the meeting to make some specific contribution to it: a report, an update, or some sort of brief presentation that is relevant to the meeting.

- Have people come prepared with their opinion (in written statement form) about at least one agenda item.

Here are some of the roles Ruth Sizemore House suggests in The Human Side of Project Management (New York: Addison-Wesley, 1988):

- *The official historian.* This person gives a brief history or summary of the last meeting and clearly states the purpose(s) of the present meeting. This way everyone attending clearly knows the reason for calling the meeting.

- *The official conscience.* This individual encourages everyone to participate, to state their feelings and opinions. He or she helps to prevent a few people from dominating the meeting.

- *The gatekeeper.* This person helps to keep the meeting focused on the subject. Sometimes people will purposely or inadvertently stray from the meeting topic. The gatekeeper has the authority to interrupt and say: "Excuse me, but we've gotten off the topic. I'll note what we've just begun to discuss and perhaps we can talk about it at our next meeting."

- *The official timekeeper.* This person is vested with the responsibility of keeping the meeting moving along and on time.

Caution: For this role-playing idea to work, it is important for your meeting participants to agree to the concepts up front. Don't try to force these roles on them.

Running Effective Meetings

#118

Use an extended agenda.

Most meeting agendas are routine. They don't tell you much about the meeting and many times are put together hastily.

The following tips suggest the items an extended agenda may contain.

#119

Be sure to list the meeting's primary purpose.

As you know, a meeting may have many purposes, but where should the real focus be? What do you want to have accomplished when the meeting is over?

#120

Estimate the time needed for each agenda item and allot that much time on the agenda.

Prior to the meeting, ask the presenter how much time he or she will need to present and discuss the topic. Always encourage the presenter to begin summarizing about three to five minutes before the end of the allotted time.

#121

Brief people before meetings about what they'll be called on to present.

If you are a supervisor or meeting leader, don't surprise people. Some managers say they do this on purpose. They say that it keeps people on their toes. Not true. It wastes time, puts people on edge, and causes them to not want to attend meetings. Have you ever been sitting in a meeting when the meeting leader surprised you—that is, called on you to make a presentation that you didn't know you were going to be called upon to make?

You may remember the experience going something like this:

"Sue, tell us about the finance project."

Surprise!

Sue says, "Well, gosh, gee, uh, it seems to be going fine."

Now how helpful is that to everyone? It would have been better to speak to Sue prior to the meeting and ask her to make a brief presentation at the next meeting.

#122

If you are making a presentation, know on whose behalf you are speaking and the purpose of your presentation.

On whose behalf are you speaking? And what is the purpose or intended outcome of your presentation? By defining these key considerations, you are likely to be more focused on productivity and results.

#123

Distribute handouts before the meeting.

Do you go to meetings where you see the handouts for the first time after you get to the meeting? Often you are expected to make an informed decision on information you never saw prior to the meeting.

The scenario usually goes something like this: "You'll note the Personnel Report in front of you. I know you are seeing it for the first time today. If you would thumb through it, perhaps we can make a quick decision on how to proceed."

Then everyone frantically reads through the report. Unfortunately, meeting participants can't digest all the information and are forced into an uninformed decision.

If someone springs a report on you in a meeting and expects you to make an immediate decision that you feel uncomfortable making, be assertive. Say: "I really don't feel comfortable making a decision today. I would appreciate having a couple of days to review the report so that I can feel better informed. Can we discuss this again in two days?"

Purpose of Meeting: To discuss decrease in market share in Widget Division Time: 10:00 a.m. – 11:45 a.m.					
Agenda Item	Time Allotment	Presenter	Client/Customer	Intended Purpose/ Outcome	Handouts
Decrease in market share–Widget Division	30 min.	DeAnn Thompson Brian Cane	Widget Division Heads	Problem Solving	Sales Figures Report
Review of 2nd Qtr. sales figures	30 min.	Bob Sheraton	All of us	Information	2nd Qtr. Report
Status report on new computer system	20 min.	Phil Baron	Data Processing	Update and Decision	Flow Chart
Discussion of sales brochure	20 min.	Sue Metz	Ed B. Sales Director	Decision	Sample Sales Brochure
Personnel	10 min.	Rob Borrow	All of us	Information	None

Figure 17. Example of an extended agenda.

YOU TRY IT!

Exercise 8: Planning an Extended Meeting Agenda

Try planning your next meeting using an extended agenda. The meeting will run more smoothly and will be a great deal more productive.

Make a copy of the extended agenda format on this page.
(If you aren't responsible for planning meetings, give this exercise to someone who is and encourage that person to try it.)

Note that there is space for five agenda items. It's unlikely that you can discuss more than that within a given meeting unless they are all information items.

> *"History repeats itself because each generation refuses to read the minutes of the last meeting."*
>
> Anonymous

Purpose of meeting:

Time: Beginning at _____ Ending at_____

Agenda Item	Time Allotment	Presenter	Client/ Customer	Intended Purpose/ Outcome	Handouts
1.					
2.					
3.					
4.					
5.					

Parkinson's Law says that "work expands to fill the time available." This is certainly true about meetings. Use an organized agenda with time allotted for each item. Also have a beginning and ending time for the whole meeting.

Some Other Great Meeting Tips

#124

Set an example by being prepared.

Regardless of how others might act or how you might feel about the meeting, go into it with a positive attitude and be well-prepared.

- Rehearse your presentation before the meeting if you are scheduled to make one.

- Be sure that you have given others the information they need to review prior to the meeting.

- If you have been given information, read and study it before the meeting. Prepare your questions and comments and attach them to the document you studied. Print attachments or use Post-it™ notes to jot down your thoughts.

- Keep your comments brief. He who is brief is invited back.

- Listen attentively when others are speaking. Taking notes will help you be more focused.

- Of course, be on time and stay on time.

#125

Have someone record meeting decisions and accountability (follow-up tasks) within 24 to 48 hours of the meeting. Distribute a meeting summary.

Summarize the meeting right away while the decisions and tasks are fresh in everyone's mind. Call the document the "Meeting Summary." It shouldn't be longer than two pages.

- List all key decisions that were made.

- Indicate those who volunteered for tasks or who were delegated tasks to complete before the next meeting. Remind meeting participants of their accountability.

- Indicate the date and place of the next meeting.

- Include handouts or attachments that are pertinent to the last meeting's agenda (Example: a list of accounting firms—based on the discussion in the last meeting—that you need to contact for your yearly audit).

Don't confuse the meeting summary with the meeting minutes. You are probably familiar with minutes. They are usually shuffled and reshuffled to the bottom of the mail pile when you receive them. A meeting summary is different from minutes.

Meeting minutes are the formal record of meeting proceedings. They are usually quite lengthy and go into some detail. It is a good idea to keep meeting minutes on file to verify and document meeting decisions. However, they usually take a while to transcribe and, consequently, they aren't distributed to meeting participants in a timely fashion.

Use the meeting summary to provide information quickly and concisely.

The High Cost of Meetings

#126

To keep meetings purposeful and to a minimum, compute the real costs of meetings.

Sometimes just the surface level costs are considered—the cost of equipment, coffee, and supplies. What is probably your most expensive cost associated with the meeting? People. The salaries of the people who are sitting in that room are the real expenses. If the meeting is not interesting and productive, you might as well be throwing money down a sewer.

Consider the following table to determine how expensive meetings are.

From the chart, you can begin to see how expensive meetings can be. For example, if you have a boring, unprepared speaker at a meeting that a staff of fifty attends, you can see the costs add up. Assume that the average salary of those in attendance is $20,000 a year ($11.90 per hour x 50 people = $595 of unproductive time). Now think about the number of hours a week you spend in meetings. This is not to say that all time in meetings is unproductive, but a conservative estimate is that at least half of it is likely to be.

Average Annual Salary of Meeting Attendees	Each Hour is Worth	Each Minute is Worth	One Hour Per Day for a Year
$15,000	$8.93	$.15	$2,143
$20,000	$11.90	$.20	$2,856
$25,000	$14.88	$.25	$3,571
$30,000	$17.86	$.30	$4,286
$35,000	$20.83	$.35	$5,000
$40,000	$23.81	$.40	$5,714
$45,000	$26.78	$.45	$6,429
$50,000	$29.76	$.50	$7,143

Source: Naylor, Harold. *How To Make Time Work For You.* Beaufort Books, 1981.

Study on how much time upper managers spend in meetings each week.

Average time spent in meetings per week: 17 hours

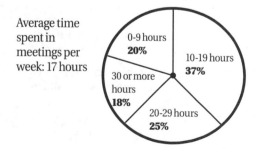

0-9 hours **20%**
10-19 hours **37%**
30 or more hours **18%**
20-29 hours **25%**

Source: Heidrick and Struggles. Reported in the *Wall Street Journal,* July 27, 1987.

Another study, by the personnel agency Accountemps, points out that we spend 72 minutes a day or 288 hours each year in meetings.

Meeting Logistics

Meeting logistics often subtly determine whether a meeting will be successful. How is the meeting room prepared for maximum productivity? Do you have the resources in the room set up to be efficient and productive?

If you want your meetings to be successful, there are three very important areas to consider as you set them up. Keep these suggestions in mind every time you plan a meeting.

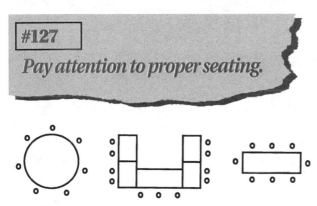

#127

Pay attention to proper seating.

Give people plenty of room. If they are crammed together, they become agitated, and sometimes they don't even know why. Also try to have comfortable chairs.

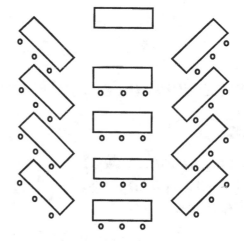

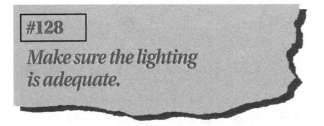

Figure 18. Seating arrangements to accommodate various meeting styles.

Each of the room set-up styles in Figure 18 are great for enhancing communication. Participants can see and can hear one another. For larger, more formal meetings, try arranging tables and chairs in a conference style.

#128

Make sure the lighting is adequate.

Figure 19. Possible seating arrangements for large, formal meetings and conferences.

Get as much lighting in the room, from either a natural or an internal source, as possible. Light has a positive effect on peoples' moods. (You may have to turn lights down for audiovisual presentations.)

Note the chevron (v-shaped) style of seating. This allows everyone to focus attention on the center of the room. It's great for larger meetings and conferences, particularly training sessions that use audiovisual aids.

#129

Try to get the meeting room temperature just right.

It is usually too warm or too cool. As a participant, always take a sweater with you to the meeting room (even in the summer). It's hard to be productive when you're too cold. If the room is too warm and you can't adjust the temperature, take frequent breaks. Better yet, find another meeting room.

#130

Be sure to furnish the meeting room with the proper accessories.

" ... Be the first to move for adjournment; this will make you popular, it's what everyone is waiting for."

Harry Chapman

Do you ever attend meetings that are regularly interrupted because no one thought of the visual aids that would be needed? Sometimes these are things as simple as flip charts or magic markers. The discussion in Chapter 8 points out how project meetings often utilize visual aids to show work breakdown structures and flow charts. Think about your meetings. What will you need?

Remember that many people learn visually. You can enhance their learning and retention if you provide visual reports and display them with the proper audiovisual equipment (i.e., overhead projector, white boards or chalkboards, flip charts, videos and video player and monitors, computers and computer displays).

Alternatives to Formal Meetings

#131

In some instances, hold conference calls instead of meetings.

There's no substitute for face-to-face, eyeball-to-eyeball contact, but sometimes it may be more cost effective and productive to hold conference calls. This is particularly true if you have staff scattered around the state, region, or country.

#132

Don't have a formal meeting if a phone call will do.

As you've already learned, formal meetings are expensive and time-consuming. Be informal, if possible. Talk to people on the phone. Just be sure to have a good written agenda for your phone call.

#133

Practice Management By Walking Around as a way of reducing formal meetings.

If you plan a part of each day to be accessible to people, on your terms, you won't need to schedule as many formal meetings. You will save yourself and your co-workers time and enhance the productivity of everyone involved.

Meeting Protocol

#134

*Mind your
meeting manners.*

Here is a checklist to remind you of some behavioral considerations that help to make meetings more productive:

✓ Don't belabor your key points. Be succinct and to the point.

✓ Listen and involve yourself in the meeting discussion.

✓ Use body language to let other meeting participants know you care and are listening. Nod your head, make eye contact, and smile.

✓ Have a sense of humor. This can break meeting tension. (However, make sure it's appropriate.)

✓ Reward people for contributing. Say something like: "Thanks for your ideas," "Very good" (if you think it is), "Good thought," "That's helpful," and so forth. (Positive reinforcement encourages people to participate more.)

✓ Don't flagrantly disagree with others. (Violent disagreements are one of the greatest productivity killers in meetings.) Instead say, "I see your point of view." It doesn't mean you agree or disagree. It does mean that you respect the other person's point of view. Then, express your viewpoint. There is a greater chance that others will hear you and really listen to your thoughts or opinions if you use this technique.

✓ Don't dismiss anyone's ideas.

✓ Don't bring food into the meeting room (unless it is a breakfast, lunch, or dinner meeting).

✓ Avoid side conversations with others.

✓ Come prepared.

✓ Avoid cursing, yelling, or screaming. That type of behavior has no place in meetings.

✓ Don't interrupt another person who is speaking.

✓ Don't get up and walk out in the middle of someone's presentation.

✓ Don't discuss trivial matters. Resolve them before or after the meeting.

✓ Don't be defensive if someone doesn't like your ideas or disagrees with you (easier said than done, but really important).

✓ If you commit to do something as a result of the meeting, be sure you follow through. (Few things will help you gain greater respect than being a person of your word; nothing will garner disrespect as much as being untrustworthy because you don't follow through.)

✓ Introduce yourself to people you don't know. Take the first step.

✓ Don't read to others when you make reports. It's boring and shows that you really aren't prepared.

✓ Avoid making inappropriate or offensive comments.

✓ Be on time.

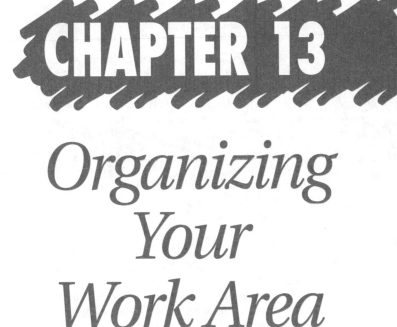

CHAPTER 13

Organizing Your Work Area and Your Paperwork

> ■■■
>
> *"Six of ten professionals pick up the same piece of paper on their desk as many as 21 times."*
>
> Study done by Fortino and Associates reported in the May 2, 1989, *Wall Street Journal*

Organizing Your Work Area

According to the study by Priority Management Pittsburgh, Inc., which was presented in Chapter 4, we spend a year of our lives looking for things we can't find. Do you sometimes feel like a magician? It was here a while ago. It just disappeared.

#135

Design your work area—at work and at home—so that everything you need is within your reach.

By arranging your work area with everything you need, you won't have to get up every five minutes to look for items you need, thus creating your own interruptions. Keep little things like paper clips, pens, pencils, your stapler, paper, a clock, stamps, your calendar, business cards, dictating equipment, scissors, and envelopes within reach.

How you arrange your work area will depend on your needs and the particulars of your job. Whether you use a desktop computer, laptop or a drafting table, for example, will affect your work area arrangement.

#136

Always keep everything in its same place.

Develop this habit so that you can easily find what you are looking for. If you keep your stapler in your upper left-hand drawer, always keep it there. This particularly applies if you travel frequently. If you don't have a system of organization and you are away from your work area for long periods, you can waste a great deal of time reacquainting yourself with your work area when you get back from your business trips.

"79% of what we do in offices is dictated by habit, not by need."

Peter Drucker

Filing Systems: Tools to Help You Organize

#137

Computerize, if possible.

You probably are aware of the wide array of software programs that are available for just about any computer application you can think of. There are countless software programs available for desktop and laptop computers.

While a computer is not a panacea (it's still up to you to get organized), it can help you with the storage and retrieval of data. Probably one of its biggest advantages, in terms of documentation, is that it can store your letters and documents as templates. You need only to make minor changes when you want to send a new letter to someone else. (This used to be called "boilerplate copy"—copy you could use over and over again.)

#138

Use a filing system, but don't depend on a central filing system.

Central filing systems are useful for keeping track of much of the company information, and they help you keep your work area from becoming cluttered. But depending entirely on a central filing system will likely negatively affect your productivity. Why?

Who owns the central filing system? Usually a secretary or "bureaucrat." This person files according to a system that you may not know. And when you go to seek information, is that person always there—or on a break, on the telephone, out sick, or just plain too busy to help you? The person who is waiting to receive the information from you can't get it unless you can figure out the filing system. And that's going to take you a while. In the meantime, your client, customer, or co-worker is thinking that you are disorganized.

#139

Keep a set of "frequently referred to" files close to your desk.

Keep paper files at arm's length, and organize your most often used electronic files for easy desktop access. These files do not need to be extensive or follow an elaborate system, but they should include information you know you will need often—perhaps pricing information and product features, benefits, and specifications.

For example, a seminar trainer may receive calls from potential clients who want to know about the course content of the trainer's seminars. Since the trainer can anticipate these calls, he or she can keep course outlines in the most accessible means possible. As the caller is asking questions, the trainer can look up the information immediately, without putting the caller on hold or calling back later.

Anticipate what you will need and be prepared.

Staying on Top of Your Reading

#140

Keep printed and electronic "reader files."

Do you receive a lot of periodicals from the various professional organizations you belong to? And does a lot of other information that must be read come across your desk or in your e-mail each day—meeting minutes, new policies and procedures, articles of interest (usually to someone else), handbooks, direct mail pieces, and other business-related items?

Start reader files. Keep the printed items you need to read, and "bookmark" on-line articles, posts and other items to easily get back to them later.

Perhaps you already have a reading file. It's probably about two inches thick. Your goal used to be to get it down to nothing. Now your goal is just to "stay on top of it"—to be in control of it.

Try this: Take it with you wherever you go. For instance, if you go to a doctor's appointment scheduled for 3:00 p.m. and arrive a few minutes early or find that the doctor is running late, pull out your reading file or check what you recently bookmarked on-line.

Likewise, think about the number of times you've arrived at the airport to catch a flight but find that the plane is late. If you have your reader file with you, you can do some catching up. Even if the plane takes off on time, you can read during the flight.

You see the point. Keep your reader file with you to stay in control of paperwork and electronic files rather than letting them control you. Use your downtime to read the important stuff in your life.

Another suggestion for using your reader file efficiently is to take it with you to the meeting room five minutes before the meeting is to begin. Chances are the meeting won't begin until 10 minutes after the assigned time. You have just given yourself 15 minutes to read from your reader file or revisit a saved on-line article, thus using this down time productively.

Don't get the wrong idea and think that you should become a workaholic and that you should be reading from your reader file every time you have down time. Sometimes you may just want to relax. Or if you're on an airplane or subway, you might want to talk with the person next to you. Or you may decide to look at a magazine in the doctor's office. The key point, though, is that if you start a reading file and always take it with you, you'll always have the reader file as an option.

A couple of tips: Do you have a chair, shelf, or credenza that your periodicals are piling up on? Do you watch the stack grow each day and say to yourself: "Someday I'm going to read those. Maybe I'll take some of them with me when I go on vacation." Bad idea.

Throw them away. Start anew! If you haven't read them up to now, you probably aren't going to.

As you start fresh, apply the "rip and read" technique. When a periodical from one of your professional organizations arrives in the mail, look at the table of contents. Determine what you really need and want to read. Rip these articles out of the magazine and put them in your reader file. Throw away the magazine. That way, you will read what you think is important and eliminate the clutter problem that causes you to lose things, thus decreasing your productivity.

Other Files to Consider

#141

Keep a project file for every one of your major projects.

For each of your important projects, keep a separate project file that contains all the information relevant to the project. On the inside front cover of the file folder, list all the activities or work packages and due dates for the project. Also list any work packages that have been assigned to other people so you can schedule follow-up.

If you are accustomed to using bar charts, staple a copy of the bar chart to the inside front cover of the file folder. Be sure to update the bar chart if the project work packages or activities change.

(This tip can be easily applied to a digital project management file system.)

Consider these three tips for using your filing system more productively:

1. Note the file category on the top right-hand corner of any document that you read. This way you won't have to reread it to see where it should be filed if you won't be filing it until later.

2. Indicate in the upper right-hand corner the date the document may be discarded. This keeps your files free of outdated materials.

3. Record the date every time you look at the document so that you can track how often you use and review the document. If you notice that a document contains many dates of reference, you may want to move it to someplace more accessible.

#142

Use a 31-day tickler file.

Buy an accordion folder that has thirty-one permanently attached folders inside, one for each day of the month. On a piece of paper, note any activity that you must follow up on and drop it into the appropriate day slot in the tickler file. Then make a note on your day planner.

Example: You receive a memo you don't need to respond to until the 15th of the next month. Because there is no need for you to act on it now, put the memo in the fifteenth slot in your tickler file. Then turn to Day 15 (for instance May 15) in your day planner and make a note to yourself that says "See tickler file today for response to memo." Now you have a convenient way to remind yourself of work that must get done. It is less likely to fall through the cracks.

If you are a supervisor, using a tickler system is a great way to follow up on your staff's tasks. It provides you with an organized system for tracking their progress, and because you are organized, you will be less likely to let something slip by.

Your commitment to following up will demonstrate to your employees that you care about the project and their roles in it. They also will know that you won't forget to follow up.

(This tip can be easily applied to a digital project management file system.)

Keeping Your Files Up to Date

#143

Weed your files at least once a year.

There is probably some point during the year that is a bit slower for you than other times. Pick a date during one of these slow times and designate it "file cleaning day" on your day planner.

For instance, if your business slows down during the winter holiday season, pick a date during that time to be file cleaning day. If your business is a little slower in the summer, then that's when you should choose your date. If you can weed twice a year, that's even better.

Here are a couple of other ideas for keeping your files free of information that you no longer need:

• Indicate on a Post-it™ note the date on which a piece of mail (or sometimes a whole file) should be discarded. If you want, write the date in red ink so it stands out.

• Use color-coded file folders to indicate short-term files.

"A file is a place to lose things alphabetically."

#144

Sponsor a "Super Saturday" for catching up on paperwork.

Ask everyone to come to work in casual attire to houseclean their files and to catch up on paperwork. Management should provide a free lunch and other incentives. If possible, designate a normal work day to do this. Be inventive. Call it "Dirt Day," "Attack Back," or something else that's catchy.

Handling the Mail

#145

Control your daily mail with the "PIG" system.
Sort your mail into three piles:

P riority—Must be handled today

I mportant—Needs to be reviewed, but not urgent

G lut—What is glut?

You guessed it. Junk mail! Which of these three piles will probably be the largest? The GLUT pile.

Perhaps you can already see the psychological advantage to separating mail. When you have just one big stack facing you, it looks as if it will take forever to review it all. But once you break your mail down, you realize that the largest stack, the glut, won't take long to go through. Concentrate your real efforts on the priority and important mail.

Hint: This idea works best if you have someone else, perhaps a secretary, sort the mail into the three piles. If you work on your own, use common sense. Is it more efficient to open each piece as you pick it up rather than to sort it first? You decide.

#146

Open your mail at the same time everyday, if possible.

Again, systematize and create your routine. It will make you more efficient. You choose the time—first thing in the morning, 10:00 a.m., right before noon, or any other time that works well for you.

Suggestion: Try keeping your mail in your top left-hand desk drawer. Have your secretary put the mail there after it is sorted. If it is urgent mail that must be acted on right away, have your secretary leave it on your desk. You'll find that the system works beautifully. Keeping the mail out of sight and acting on it at the same time each day will help you to be more productive.

#147

Do not keep an "in" basket on your desk.

If you do, it will beckon you. Your mail will seem to say, "Open me, open me." It will distract you when you should be working on a high-payoff activity.

Keep your "in" basket out of your direct line of sight—on a shelf, cabinet, credenza, or somewhere else that is within easy reach (where you don't have to get up). Keep your "out" basket there too.

Here's another acronym for you to remember: TAME the paper tiger.

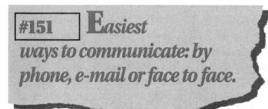

#148 **T**oss
what you don't need.

It just creates clutter. No, you probably won't need it six months from now. If you think you will, keep it in the organization's central filing system.

#149 **A**ct
on all paper immediately.

That is, decide to do something with it—respond to it, file it, throw it away, or pass it on. Use the "chicken pox method" to keep from looking at mail over and over. Each time you look at a piece of paper, put a dot (preferably red) in its upper right-hand corner. If the paper has several red dots, you know you have a problem. Ask yourself, "What is preventing me from taking action?" Then do something about it.

#150 **M**ake
notes on correspondence that requires follow-up.

Indicate to yourself what you need to do with a piece of paper if you are not responding to it or passing it along immediately.

Tip: With internal memos, it's usually appropriate to write a handwritten reply on the memo and then return it to the sender. Your response will be immediate and you won't tie up your time or your secretary's time typing a formal response.

#151 **E**asiest
ways to communicate: by phone, e-mail or face to face.

In other words, don't write when a phone call or personal conversation will do. In fact, the latter is preferable.

Cover your tracks. In some offices, everyone sends memos to each other—even co-workers who sit right next to one another. They do this to document everything they say and do. The message that is really sent is "I don't trust you." Before sending a memo to cover your tracks, be sure to ask, "Is a memo really necessary?" Again, use common sense.

What about reading all that mail?

There are some excellent speed reading courses available. You might want to take one. Here are some suggestions for plowing through all that mail and paperwork:

#152
Read for speed.

- *Scan:* Read the first and last paragraphs to determine the purpose of the memo. (Unfortunately, not all writers will clearly state their purpose, but if they do, you will most likely find it in one of these two paragraphs.)

- *Read:* Read the first sentence of each paragraph—or the first two sentences if it is a long paragraph. Use a highlighter to help you focus on key points.

- *Guide:* Use your pen or pencil to "fast pace" yourself through the reading material. More than likely, your eyes will move faster to keep pace with your pen or pencil, or you will learn to read faster.

- *Study:* This is detailed reading. It may be necessary to study important reports, directions, and instructions. Make your own notes in the margins.

Writing Letters and Memos for Productivity and Results

According to the *Training and Development Journal*, the publication of the American Society for Training and Development, the average cost of a business letter today is an astounding $100.

When you are writing letters or memos:

#153

Keep them brief and to the point.

What do you do with a three- or four-page memo when it shows up in your stack of mail? If you are like most people, you put it back on the bottom of the stack to read "when you have more time." So, if you want others to read your memos and letters, keep them brief and to the point.

#154

As a general rule, keep your correspondence to one page or less.

Keeping your correspondence concise will save you and your reader time. Your key points will likely be more clearly stated and discernible, and there is a much greater chance that your correspondence will be read. (There are some exceptions to the one-page rule. Sometimes documentation or instructional letters will be lengthier, but even then, concentrate on brevity.)

#155

Get to the point assertively. In the first paragraph, state why you are writing.

Your first paragraph should be your "grabber" paragraph that causes your reader to want to read on. Keep your paragraphs brief. Don't lump your thoughts together in one paragraph. Doing so makes your letter or memo look intimidating, and it is harder to read and to separate the key points and ideas.

#156

Explain what you want your readers to do as a result of reading your letter.

What action is required? Be specific and be sure to indicate definite deadlines. Don't use terms like "as soon as possible" or "at your convenience." State clearly what action you want your readers to take and by when.

"As soon as possible" (ASAP) is one of the most confusing directives used in business. "As soon as possible" has little, if any, meaning. Don't ask people to respond to you ASAP. Their perspective may well be different than yours. You may mean you want a response by the end of the day. But to your reader, ASAP may mean tomorrow afternoon. If you want others to understand and take action by a certain time, be specific.

#157

Only send copies (CCs) to those who really need to be informed.

According to a study conducted by Accountemps, we spend 32 minutes a day writing unnecessary memos. That equates to 128 hours a year, or more than three work weeks a year.

A study based on interviews with vice presidents and personnel directors of 100 of the nation's largest corporations found that:

- The average executive spends 22 percent of his or her time writing or reading memos. (That's 11 work weeks a year.)
- They believed that 39 percent of all memos are unnecessary and wasteful.
- 76 percent said that most memos were too long.
- 58 percent thought that copies were routed to too many people.

Source: Half, Robert, "Memomania." *American Way.*
November 1, 1989, pp. 21-24.

Some organizations have full-fledged "memo wars." Employees strive to see who can send the most memos and how many people they can send copies to. These "missiles" waste everyone's time. One of the reasons so many copies are sent is related to covering your tracks: "I must document everything I do so that everyone knows" and "I can't trust anyone to follow through on anything, so I'd better put everything in writing."

#158

Dictate rather than write.

Dictation is a skill that needs to be learned. It takes practice. Purchase a digital dictating machine or mobile app. If you are a salesperson or in another profession that requires car travel, you can dictate reports, letters, and memos while driving between appointments. (Don't try to dictate in city traffic.) You can also stop your car and take minibreaks to record your memos and ideas. Another option, of course, is to add dictation software to your desktop or laptop computer. (They are discussed in Chapter 17.)

If you dictate in your office, you will be able to compose letters much more quickly than when you write or type them. Keep in mind that if you aren't currently using dictating equipment, it may take some time to become adept at using it. At first you might think that it's easier to write or type letters, but keep practicing how to dictate effectively. Once you learn to dictate, you will see how it enhances your productivity.

Hint: Avoid dictating directly to a secretary. Although this is no longer a common practice, it's still worth a reminder. When you dictate to a secretary, you are, of course, keeping that person from spending time on high-payoff pursuits. Dictate into the electronic device, and let your secretary transcribe from your dictation.

Dealing With Electronic Mail

Electronic mail (e-mail) has, for the most part, replaced handwriting or printed paper messages in recent years.

The myriad of options to access, send, and proliferate messages across internal intranets and the Internet has been both an opportunity for greater productivity and a source of abuse depending on how it is used. Much of what has already been discussed in this book about written communication also applies to e-mail.

Here are some additional key points to remember:

#159

Keep e-mail messages as brief as possible.

Because e-mail is so convenient to use, people can send dozens of messages each day without ever leaving their work areas. Co-workers can be inundated with all of these messages. Have respect for those receiving your messages by keeping them brief.

#160

Control e-mail by working in time chunks.

This book has emphasized working in time blocks to answer phone messages, handle correspondence, and so forth—the same thing goes with your e-mail messages. Review your computer messages at specific times during the day rather than continually.

#161

Answer electronic mail messages as you access them.

Take time to respond to your e-mail messages during the same chunk of time you review them. Don't wait until much later, after more messages have piled up. You'll waste time reading the earlier messages to remind yourself what they were about.

#162

Keep a correspondence file.

Maintain a file that contains a copy of every piece of correspondence you send: formal letters, memos, and handwritten notices. Organize it chronologically.

Here are your alternatives:

- **Manual file.** Keep all paper correspondence in file folders.

- **Computer file.** Store all letters, important e-mails and memos generated by computer.

- **Combination of manual and computer file.** This combination is a practical alternative for many of today's businesses. Keep formal letters and memos in secure electronic folders. Use a manual file to maintain handwritten correspondence.

Here are two advantages to keeping a correspondence file:

1. It serves as a referral for future letters you must write. Why "reinvent the wheel" or start from scratch? Many times you can use approximately the same body of a letter. If you have it on file, you merely need to reference it and modify it for your new letter.

2. It is a documentation source. Here's where covering your tracks comes into the picture again. If you must document a letter you sent, a decision you made, a problem you solved, or some other situation, you will have a record of it in your correspondence file. Keeping your letters and memos on file is better than sending copies at random to everyone in the department or organization to routinely acquaint them with everything you do.

CHAPTER 14

Dealing With Procrastination

> "Whatever you do, do it with all your might. Work at it early and late, in season and out of season, not leaving a stone unturned and never deferring for a single hour that which can be done just as well now."
>
> P.T. Barnum

Reasons People Procrastinate

To put procrastination into perspective, consider this definition from Don Marquis. He said that procrastination is the art of keeping up with yesterday. Unfortunately, being a day late may well be the difference between success and failure.

Why do people procrastinate?

- **The task seems overwhelming.** The procrastinator's perspective is that the task is too big and too cumbersome and will take too long to accomplish. The procrastinator thinks, "When will I ever have time to tackle this job?"

- **The activity is unpleasant.** You just don't want to do the task—it's boring or considered low payoff or too difficult.

- **The final "rush" to meet a deadline is a kind of "high."** Think back to college or high school and those term papers that you put off until the night before. You probably psyched yourself up and stayed up half the night writing, drinking coffee, and taking No-Doz. Not a good idea! But remember the feeling of that last-minute rush? You may have started a habit that you now find hard to break.

- **There is no immediate payoff.** If you complete the task now, you may not receive any immediate reward. In our society, we are used to receiving immediate gratification. We tend to think "If I can't have results now, I'm not going to do it until later."

- **It might go away.** And you know what? Occasionally it does. Sometimes if we wait long enough, the unpleasant task will become unimportant and unnecessary. Or, sometimes a problem that needs to be solved seemingly solves itself. Occasionally, a decision that needs to be made is made by someone else.

The problem goes away just often enough to validate to the procrastinator that not taking action is a rational option. Guess what? It's not. If people live their lives on the assumption that the problem will go away, they are in for a lifetime of disappointment and failure.

> *"Knowest the true value of time. Snatch, seize and enjoy every moment of it. No idleness, no laziness, no procrastination. Never put off till tomorrow what you can do today."*
>
> Lord Chesterfield

Other reasons for procrastination:

- **Perfectionism.** The job never gets done because it isn't perfect. You know what? It never will be. But perfectionists can never take action to get results because they never feel that what they are doing is good enough. Some people pride themselves on being perfectionists. They brag about their behavior, but they seldom get the job done. Do a job well, with excellence, not with perfection. If you strive for perfection, you will never see results. Remember, excellence is doing the right things right.

According to a study conducted by James Fields, a respected management consultant, the average employee is productive only 55 percent of the time. How do people waste the rest of their time?

- Fifteen percent is lost to personal time.

- Thirty percent is related to scheduling problems, unclear assignments, improper staffing, and poor discipline. People procrastinate.

Procrastination behavior is a bad habit that develops over a period of time. Discipline to follow through by gaining commitment, direction, and adequate resources can help overcome the problem.

- **Fear of success.** Some people fear success. They see it as bringing greater pressure, more notoriety, and, thus, more headaches. They may subconsciously program themselves not to achieve success. They sabotage their success by procrastinating.

- **Fear of failure.** Fear of failure may be the biggest reason of all for procrastination. Procrastinators can actually see themselves failing. They create a false impression in their minds of themselves failing.

False
Evidence
Appearing
Real

Procrastinators sometimes paint vivid pictures of how they will fail. They can become so fearful of being associated with the task that they become immobilized.

Action
Creates
Triumph

They find every excuse to put off taking action. Procrastinators who project failure must change the way they see life. Instead of visualizing failure, they must change their perspective to see what they can accomplish so that they will ACT.

"One of these days is none of these days."

Big Al Juodikis

Overcoming Procrastination Behavior

Deal with procrastination NOW!

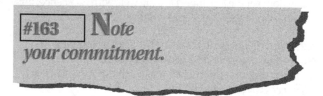

#163 **N**ote *your commitment.*

Note your commitment to yourself first. That is what the first section of this book is really all about: noting your commitment to yourself by writing out goals that result in activities that you noted on your "To Do" list and in your day planner.

Note your commitment to others. Tell co-workers, friends, or a relative about an action you plan to take. Example: If you are considering quitting smoking, set a definite date for beginning, and then tell several friends or associates about it. Let them become your support system. One word of caution: Noting your commitment to others is not the same as "shooting off your mouth" frivolously with no intent to follow through.

#164 **O**wn *the project or task.*

We tend to take better care of the things we own. Not every task or activity can be exciting and stimulating, but try to be sure that some of what you do each day is truly of your own choice. And see if there is a way to make the less interesting tasks more interesting.

The more you can make your work interesting, the more exciting your work will be. For tasks that you must just "get through," be sure to commit to them on your day planner. As Wilfred Peterson said, "Happiness doesn't come from doing what we like to do but from liking what we have to do."

George "PaPa Bear" Halas once said, "Nothing is work unless you would rather be doing something else." Isn't it true? Activities that interest you don't seem so much like work. You're even willing to work late if you are in the middle of an interesting and exciting project. The more you can own a task, the more you will commit to it.

#165 **W**ork *in small steps.*

This is the real key to overcoming procrastination. Break tasks into subtasks. Remember the concept of work breakdown structures and work packages that was discussed in Chapter 8.

Goals → Objectives → Activities

The activities are the small steps we take to achieve the entire goal or project over a designated period of time.

"Never put off until tomorrow what you can do the day after tomorrow."

Mark Twain

Additional Tips For Putting an End to Procrastination

Here are some other thoughts to help you cross the finish line successfully:

#166

Delegate some of the tasks.

Enlist others to help you complete some of the activities or work packages. (You'll find a more complete discussion of delegation in Chapter 18.)

#167

Reward yourself for your "mini-completions."

Congratulate yourself when you achieve a step toward accomplishing your goal or project. Reward yourself.

#168

Start today—now—to do something about procrastination.

Don't procrastinate overcoming procrastination. Use Exercise 9 to do something about it now!

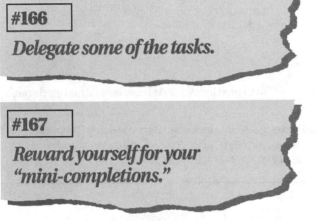

***YOU* TRY IT!**

Exercise 9: Overcoming Procrastination

Two things I've been procrastinating about:

1. _____

2. _____

Start date for item #1 _____ The person to whom I'll commit: _____

Start date for item #2 _____ The person to whom I'll commit: _____

Now, put these tasks on your "To Do" list and commit to them on your day planner.

Break the habit of procrastination in order to enhance your productivity.

Here are some suggestions about procrastination from Dr. Wayne Dyer's book *Your Erroneous Zones*:

- Live 15 minutes at a time. (Plan for the future, but live it out today to the best of your ability. Concentrate on the moment.)

- Start something you've been postponing.

- Designate a specific time for a task you've been postponing.

- Look hard at your life. Are you doing what you would choose to do if you had six months to live? (What's really important?)

- Decide not to be tired until the moment before you get into bed. (Is it possible that we talk ourselves into being tired because following through is boring, too difficult, or may subject us to failure?)

- Eliminate the words *hope, wish, should,* and *maybe* from your vocabulary. (They are all powerless words, words of noncommitment.)

How many times have you overheard someone say this during lunch: "I'm so tired today. I don't know how I'll make it through this afternoon. Gosh, I hate to go back to work."

People who complain day after day about how tired they are had better take a close look at what they're doing. These kind of statements are a sign of boredom, fatigue, or burnout. Overcome this syndrome by taking control and ownership of your day and your life. Plan for excitement and meaningfulness by defining what you want each day in your life.

Be persistent in overcoming procrastination.

Stay with tasks that need to be accomplished. Avoid human barriers, particularly people who might tell you to give up. Consider the following poem by Edgar A. Guest.

It Couldn't Be Done

Somebody said that it couldn't be done,
But he with a chuckle replied.

That "maybe it couldn't," but he would be one
Who wouldn't say so till he'd tried.

So he buckled right in with the trace of a grin
On his face. If he worried, he hid it.

He started to sing as he tackled the thing
That couldn't be done, and he did it.

Somebody scoffed, "Oh, you'll never do that;
At least no one ever has done it."

But he took off his coat and he took off his hat,
And the first thing we knew, he'd begun it.

With a lift of his chin and a bit of a grin,
Without any doubting or quiddit.

He started to sing as he tackled the thing
That couldn't be done, and he did it.

There are thousands to tell you it cannot be done,
There are thousands to prophesy failure;

There are thousands to point out to you, one by one,
The dangers that wait to assail you.

But buckle in with a bit of a grin,
Just take off your coat and go to it;

Just start to sing as you tackle the thing
That "cannot be done" and you'll do it.

CHAPTER 15

Working Effectively With Your Supervisor

The difference between a boss and a leader:

The boss drives employees; the leader coaches them.

The boss depends on authority; the leader on goodwill.

The boss inspires fear; the leader generates enthusiasm.

The boss says "I"; the leader says "We."

The boss places blame for the breakdown; the leader fixes the breakdown.

The boss knows how it is done; the leader shows how it is done.

The boss uses people; the leader develops people.

The boss takes credit; the leader gives credit.

The boss commands; the leader asks.

The boss says "Go"; the leader says "Let's go."

Management Style and Effect
Dave Davis

Another Obstacle to Productivity— Your Supervisor

From the employee's perspective, many times the supervisor is the biggest obstacle to productivity. Jobs aren't clearly communicated, priorities aren't established, managers can't or won't make decisions, and the manager doesn't see the employee's perspective.

This is not to pick on supervisors or to make all of them appear to be "those horrible, terrible people" on the other side. Some of you are supervisors. And most of you know that most supervisors aren't trying to make life difficult for their employees.

The real issue here, in terms of productivity, is perspective.

In the following scenario are two well-meaning people who see life from two totally different perspectives. Unless they begin to really communicate, they are both headed for trouble and possible failure.

Supervisor's Perspective

Your Perspective
(What you would LIKE to say.)

"Sharon, I really think we can have this project done within six months if no one gets sick, if we don't have any turnover, if everyone shows up on time, if we have no equipment failure, and if the weather cooperates. Yeah, if nothing goes wrong, we should be able to do this job in six months."

"Six months! Are you out of your mind? There's no way we can complete this project in six months—maybe in nine months, and that's pushing it. If you want six months, then you're going to have to give me more human resources and budget. Six months, huh? You must believe in fairy tales."

What you actually do say.

"Well, Mrs. Phillips, I'll try to get it done, but I'll have to juggle some of my other projects around."

(Translation: I'll have to come in early, stay late, work through my breaks, and shorten my lunch time. Otherwise, there's no way I can get this done in six months.)

What is the probability that nothing will go wrong? Zero, you say. You're almost right. According to probability theory (a mathematical formula), the chance that nothing will go wrong is less than 1 percent. Yet, many times, employees are beset with unrealistic parameters.

Who loses in this scenario? Both Sharon and Mrs. Phillips, but since the supervisor has the authority, the employee may well turn out to be the big loser.

Also, your supervisor's perspective may be affected by his or her own supervisor's perspective. He or she may have been given an ultimatum to "get that project done within six months or else." So, your supervisor is just following orders. Until those involved really begin to communicate, they are doomed to failure.

#169

The keys to productivity in working with your supervisor are effective communication and savvy negotiation.

Consider the results of a study conducted by a seminar firm and reported in *USA Today*.

The survey asked more than 1,000 employees to rank on-the-job problems by degree of seriousness. Here are the top five that were indicated:

Poor communication	**30%**
Excessive interruptions	**16%**
No clear-cut priorities	**10%**
Workload too heavy	**10%**
Managerial indecisiveness	**10%**

"Either lead, follow or get out of the way."

(sign on Ted Turner's desk)

Communicating With Your Supervisor

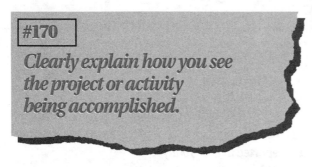

#170

Clearly explain how you see the project or activity being accomplished.

The goal is to reach a common perspective. Here are two tips for communicating with your supervisor to reach a common perspective:

#171

Concentrate on using "I" statements.

This is called "assertive communication."

Example: "I really think I can get this project done in nine months. I believe that given the resources I have and the complexity of the task, it will take longer than six months. I'll be happy to draw up a schedule and chart the project. Also, since I am working on those other three projects, a nine-month schedule will make it more likely that I will stay on schedule with all of my projects." (Note that the dialogue involves positive statements such as "I can," "I have," "I'll be happy to," "I will." "I" statements convey, from your perspective, what you *can* do.)

#172

Avoid using "you" statements in these situations. They are usually perceived as aggressive.

Example: "*You* want me to have this project done in six months! *You* know, that's going to be difficult. *You* really haven't given me enough human resources, time, or budget to do this job within six months. Also, *you* must have forgotten that you want me to complete those other three projects. *You're* really expecting a lot."

Notice the difference in the communication. In the latter instance, the communication is likely to be perceived by the supervisor as a verbal attack, and the supervisor may perceive the employee as a negative complainer. If the employee continues to use "you" language in other difficult situations, he or she may be permanently labeled as a complainer or negative influence.

Keep in mind that the "I" versus "you" concept discussed here is for trying to bring differing perspectives into a common focus.

In some life situations, "you" statements can be wonderful: You are beautiful. You do such a good job. You are right.

Conversely, some "I" statements can be a problem: I disagree. I don't buy your argument.

→

The "I" versus "you" concept is one of the most important concepts discussed in this book. Whether you are at work or at home, the idea is to communicate in a way that gets the other person to listen, to see your perspective. Likewise, try to see the other person's perspective. The goal is to reach a common perspective.

Some Other Ideas for Communicating With Your Supervisor

#173

Here are five key ideas to communicate to your supervisor to make both of you more productive:

> *"If all possible objections must first be overcome, nothing significant will ever get done."*
>
> Charles Kettering

1. **Communicate your key priorities so that your supervisor knows what you think is important.** Don't just assume that your supervisor already knows your priorities. It is also important for your supervisor to tell you what he or she considers priority. If you and your supervisor don't communicate your priorities, you may spend almost all of your time working on low-payoff items, with little opportunity for real productivity. Recall the "rationalization" quadrant of the Productivity Paradigm in Chapter 1.

2. **Communicate what else you would like to do.** You could be thinking: "Oh great. That's just what I need is more work. I'm better off keeping my mouth shut." Wrong. Explain to your supervisor what else you would like to do that interests you or that would help you learn a skill. You may, for example, have a latent talent for creative marketing. Ask to learn the company's latest desktop publishing software. Sure, learning it may be more work in the short run, but it probably will help you and those around you in the long run.

3. **Communicate what you need clarified.** Sometimes people don't ask questions because they fear that they will be considered dumb or stupid. What's really dumb is not asking—and then doing something stupid. Remember to use "I" statements. (Example: "I don't think I understand the third step. I would appreciate having it explained to me again.")

4. **Communicate what you need help with**—additional staffing or other resources, for example. Review Idea #170— you must convey to your supervisor how you see the project being accomplished, including the areas where you will need help. Savvy negotiation will help you get what you need. (See ideas #174 – 181.)

5. **Communicate deadlines.** One of the major reasons for decreased productivity is lack of deadlines or unclear deadlines. Don't make assumptions or agree to terms like "ASAP" or "next week" or "as soon as you can get around to it." You and your supervisor must be specific with each other when it comes to deadlines.

> *"Before you have an argument with your boss, take a good look at both sides—your boss's side and the outside."*
>
> Anonymous

Learn How to Negotiate for What You Need to Be Productive

Once you've used "I" statements to get your supervisor to listen to your perspective, negotiating skills become important. Here are eight negotiating skills that can help you get what you need in order to be productive and successful.* These tips won't absolutely guarantee that you'll get everything you ask for (human resources, more time, budget, equipment), but you will likely get more than you started with. If you don't become a proficient negotiator, you can pretty well count on getting nothing.

#174

Be direct.

Know what you want and ask for it. State specifically what you want using "I" statements. *Example:* "Bob, I really think I can bring this job in with quality if I can have four weeks instead of 2 1/2 weeks."

#175

Label behavior.

Example: "I will feel better explaining to my staff that they don't have to rush through this job."

#176

Avoid argument.

If the other person disagrees with your point of view and tries to coax you into an argument, resist the temptation to fight back. Remain calm. Let the other person choose anger. Throw the responsibility for justifying behavior back to the other person.

Example:

The other person: "Four weeks! Are you crazy?"
You: "No. I just think I could provide quality work with four weeks. I really need your help on this. It would help me to know why four weeks is a problem."

#177

Be aware of the limitations of logic, at least in negotiating.

Sometimes saying "I'll give up X if you will give up Y" seems logical, but it may not solve the problem or be the best solution. It may be better to arrive at a creative solution rather than a logical one.

Seven Traits Necessary for Effective Negotiators

1. Planning skills
   (Be prepared—know what you want to say.)
2. Ability to think clearly under stress
3. Common sense
4. Verbal ability (effective communication skills)
5. Program or product knowledge
6. Personal integrity
7. Ability to perceive and use power

"A good negotiator must have a good self-image, as well as a high tolerance for ambiguity and uncertainty, open mindedness, courage and a real desire to achieve, to aspire, to take that sensible but extra measure of risk that represents a commitment to one's striving."

Source: Karrass, Chester. *Negotiating Game.*
Thomas Y. Crowell Co., 1970.

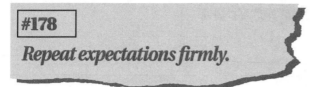

#178

Repeat expectations firmly.

There are two reasons to repeat your expectations:

1. The person you are speaking with may not have been listening to you seriously the first time you stated your expectations. After hearing the words "four weeks," the person may have tuned you out and not heard your reasoning.

2. For clarification—you need to be sure the other person received your message. A good definition of communication is that the other person received the message you intended.

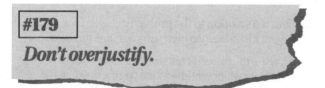

#179

Don't overjustify.

After you state your major points, don't ramble on. You may talk yourself out of "the sale" or say something that gives the other person the opportunity to poke holes in your position.

As you stop speaking, there may be silence. That can be uncomfortable—those silent moments may seem like a lifetime. But resist the temptation to speak. Let the other person respond. You have to know when to quit selling. Resisting the temptation to speak successfully illustrates the power of silence.

#180

Avoid using "negative trigger words."

These are irritating words that trigger a negative response in the other person. Avoid using the "you" statements discussed in Idea #172.

Other phrases and words to avoid:

- "You're wrong."
- "No way."
- "You need to … "
- "You're going to have to clarify that for me."
- "I disagree with you."
- "You don't understand."

#181

Create alternative solutions.

Again, be aware of the limitations of logic. Be creative when looking at alternatives for bringing your perspective and your supervisor's perspective into a common focus.

*Source for negotiating tips: Kerzner, Harold.
Project Management: A Systems Approach to Planning, Scheduling and Controlling. Van Nostrand Reinhold, 1989.

> *"Negotiation is the exchange of ideas for the purpose of influencing behavior … Wishes are converted into reality through the cold water of bargaining."*
>
> Chester Karrass

How to Get Direction From Your Supervisor in Prioritizing Your Work

#182

Clearly state what you can't do right now.

You might be thinking, "Yeah, if I do that, I won't have a job tomorrow." Remember, it's *how* you say it that counts. Tip: Use the USA method discussed in Chapter 10 for saying no when you feel overloaded. Here is how you can use USA to say, "I can't do that right now."

> **U**nderstanding statement:
> "I know that this new project you want me to do is important."
>
> **S**ituation:
> "I'm working on project A, project B, and project C."
>
> **A**ction:
> "I would appreciate your assistance in helping me schedule this new project in relation to the other three. How will this new project fit in?"

What you have said is: "Do you know I'm overloaded with work right now? I need for you to help me schedule. I want you to see life from my perspective."

You are asking your supervisor to:

*   Take action—help you to make a decision about how the new project can be scheduled with the rest of your work.
*   Take responsibility—to provide you direction.
*   Consider giving the task to someone else who may not be as busy.
*   Communicate with you so that you know his or her perspective.

If you ask your supervisor, "Which of these projects/activities/tasks is most important?" the answers you might hear are:

*   "They're all important."
*   "Just get them all done."
*   "You decide. That's what you get paid to do."
*   "I'm too busy to help you right now."

None of these answers are helpful. They give you no direction. Supervisors are often just overloaded with their own work. They are not being purposely difficult. They are seeing life from their perspective. They are in a hurry to get the work out.

Here is a solution to the problem:
Present a handwritten memo to your boss that says:

"Here are the projects I am working on for the next three months (or whatever time frame you choose) and the schedule for completing each one, as I see it:

Project A, completion date: _____ .
Project B, completion date: _____ .
Project C, completion date: _____ .

Unless I hear otherwise from you, I will work on them accordingly."

Give the note to your supervisor. You are now more likely to get your supervisor's attention. The purpose is not to create conflict, but to open communication so that you can get clarification and direction.

Be sure your note is handwritten. Keep the process informal. If you formally prepare the memo, it may put your supervisor on the defensive.

CHAPTER 16

How to Work With More Than One Supervisor

> "Nine-tenths of the serious controversies which arise in life result from misunderstanding."
>
> Louis D. Brandeis

The Tug of War

If you work for more than one person, you can be pushed, pulled, shoved, tugged, beat up, beat down, stepped on, and stressed out unless you take control of your productivity and make your supervisors responsible to each other. Consider the following scenarios:

Scenario #1

You work for Mark and Jane. Presently, you are working on a task for Jane. Mark comes up to you and asks, "What are you doing?"

You: "I'm working on Jane's project."

Mark: "Well, you'll have to set it aside. I need for you to get this report out for me right away."

Where does this leave you? In a no-win situation.

Scenario #2

You are working on Jane's project and Mark asks, "What are you working on?"

You: "Jane's project. She needs it done by the end of the day."

Mark: "Well, you tell Jane that you have to set her project aside because I need mine done by 3:30 p.m."

Where does this leave you? Again, in a no-win situation.

Solution: There is no easy solution, but there is a tough one. It requires tremendous mental fortitude on your part.

#183

Be direct and specific.

Look the other person in the eye and say: "I don't feel comfortable making that choice. I would like for you and Jane to discuss how you would like to proceed."

It is not your responsibility to:

• Fight your supervisors' battles.

• Make a decision for your supervisors that has no positive outcome for you.

• Drop everything based on someone else's lack of organization.

You could be thinking, "But if I don't do what they want, I may get fired."

Actually, if you just do what you're told, you will make the other supervisor unhappy anyway. And eventually you will be so stressed out you'll quit or get fired. Do something proactive now rather than being reactive later. Speak up in an assertive way.

> *"The firings will continue until the morale improves."*
>
> (sign in many employee offices)

Other Tips to Help You Work With More Than One Supervisor

#184

Encourage your supervisors to have face-to-face or telephone conversations with each other to discuss their priorities.

If your supervisors know what they want you to do, they can help you schedule the work, which will make all of you more productive.

#185

Ask for specific deadline dates to help you prioritize.

Be sure to get a specific date, not ASAP.

#186

Have frequent meetings with your supervisors.

Hold a 10-minute (no longer than 15-minute) meeting with your supervisors first thing each morning to outline their priorities and to give them an opportunity to communicate with each other face to face.

#187

Communicate conflict.

Don't hold it in or be afraid to speak up. If you do, you likely will be the loser. When your supervisors want their work done at the same time, let each supervisor know that there is a conflict. Find out which task has highest priority.

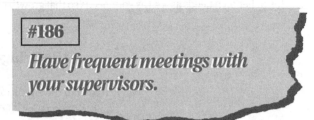

"The meetings of two personalities is like the contact of two chemical substances: if there is any reaction, both are transformed."

Carl Jung

Be a Bridge Builder

Whether you are the supervisor or the employee working with the supervisor, you have an obligation to help the other person meet his or her own needs as well as your needs so that growth can occur and so that you can each have greater productivity.

The Bridge Builder

An old man traveling a lone highway,
Came at the evening cold and gray,
To a chasm vast, deep and wide,
Through which was flowing a sullen tide,
The old man crossed in the twilight dim,
The sullen stream held no fears for him;
But he turned when safe on the other side,
And built a bridge to span the tide.
"Old man," cried a fellow pilgrim near,
"You're wasting your time in building here.
Your journey will end with the closing day;
You never again will pass this way.
You have crossed the chasm deep and wide,
Why build you this bridge at eventide?"
The builder lifted his old grey head,
"Good friend, in the path I have come," he said,
"There followeth after me today
A youth whose feet must pass this way.
This stream, which has been as naught to me,
To that fair-haired youth may pitfall be.
He, too, must cross in the twilight dim,
Good friend, I am building this bridge for him."

Allen Dromgoole

Build bridges for others to be successful. If you do, you too will probably be productive and successful.

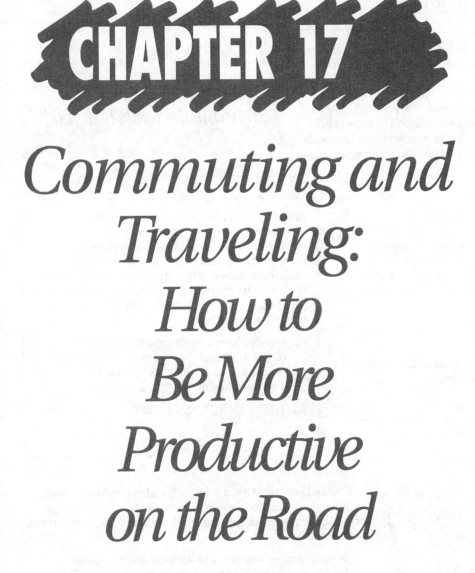

CHAPTER 17

Commuting and Traveling: How to Be More Productive on the Road

Tools for Increasing Productivity During Your Commute

If you commute to and from work or appointments, you probably are spending at least one hour a day in your car (or on the train, subway, or bus). That equates to at least 20 hours a month or 2 1/2 working days a month, which is 30 days a year. So, you spend at least one month a year commuting to and from work or appointments. And this is a conservative estimate. Many people spend far more than an hour a day commuting. Think about what you could do or learn with that time! Your car (or train or subway or bus) can become a traveling office if you prepare yourself.

> *"Everything comes to him who hustles while he waits."*
>
> Thomas Edison

The management consulting firm Priority Management Pittsburgh, Inc., sent researchers out across the country, often with a stopwatch in hand, to observe the amount of time people spent in various life situations. Then the researchers extrapolated how much time people spend over a lifetime in these various situations. Two of the findings:

1. We spend six months of our lives waiting at stoplights.

2. We spend five years of our lives waiting in lines. Use that downtime to your advantage.

In his audiobook *How to Be a No-Limit Person*, Dr. Wayne Dyer explains how he went to college at Wayne State University in Detroit. He says that everyday during his commute to school, the traffic would back up, and he would get angry and pound his fists on the steering wheel. It wasn't until many years later, he notes, that he learned two important lessons from this experience:

1. He could have used that commute time productively, perhaps listening to self-help audio programs. He lamented that he could have learned a new language during those four years.

2. THE TRAFFIC DOESN'T CARE.

#188

Listen and learn while you are in your car.

Use your downtime to listen to self-help and motivational material. Such resources abound. You can learn business concepts, foreign languages, sales techniques, organizational skills, and a multitude of other things.

And many books—even classics—are available in audio form. What a great way to spend time while sitting in the traffic. This doesn't mean that you have to spend every moment you're in the car listening to educational audio programs. You might choose to relax with the car stereo or to listen to traffic reports. Just remember that you can spend some of your time on more productive pursuits.

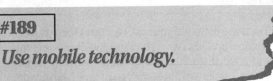

#189
Use mobile technology.

If you travel a great deal from appointment to appointment and make and receive a number of calls during the day, a mobile phone with networking capabilities will allow you to work productively even when you're not at your desk or even near your office.

Three features to consider when using a mobile phone in the car:

1. **A hands-free speaker phone.** Obviously a hands-free device is safer to use in the car.

2. **Voice-activated dialing.** Again, voice-activated dialing allows you to keep your hands on the steering wheel. You can "dial" by voice command.

3. **Memory dialing.** Most of your calls are probably to the same companies, organizations, friends, business associates, and acquaintances. Memory dialing allows you to call them by dialing just one number. And, if you have voice-activated dialing, you can "command" your phone to make the call by saying one number.

"He not being born is busy dying."

Bob Dylan

Tip: Keep Post-it™ note pads in your car and use them to write a brief agenda for any calls you will be making from your automobile. Stick them to your dashboard as a reminder of the items you wish to discuss with the people you're calling. This will help you keep your calls focused and succinct so that you will be more productive and save money.

"The time for action is now. It's never too late to do something."

Carl Sandburg

#190

Dictate while commuting.

> Tip: If you dictate in your car, be sure to keep your car window up. Otherwise, the wind and the noise of the traffic will distort the sound. The person transcribing your message will have a very hard time hearing your voice over the din of the traffic.

Isn't it amazing how many great ideas pop into your head when you're commuting? If you don't write them down or record them, you could lose them forever. Use a recording device to capture those thoughts. There are apps available for your mobile phone that record dictation, and stand-alone digital dictating devices are very compact and easy to carry with you. Not only can you record your thoughts and ideas, you can also dictate letters and memos. You can dictate about four to seven times faster than you can write longhand. And if your device has a voice-activation feature, you can record without long blank gaps.

Here are some features to consider when purchasing a recording device:

1. **A counter** that allows you to refer back to previously recorded information. Before you begin recording, note the number on the counter. That way you don't have to search at random for the ideas or letters that you record.

2. **Quick erase** so that previous material doesn't get transcribed again.

3. **Cue and review** features so that you can quickly review information you have recorded.

4. **An adapter** that will plug into your car's cigarette lighter. You'll save batteries if you purchase a device with an adapter.

If you dictate your letters and memos, they will, of course, need to be transcribed. Either you or a secretary must do this later. Be sure to have the right kind of transcribing equipment. Some of the features to look for include:

- Speed control—to slow down the recording to make it easier to transcribe.

- High-quality earphones—to listen efficiently and to block out background noise.

> While sitting in a traffic jam, Noel Coward wrote the popular song "I'll See You Again." You'd be surprised how efficiently you can use your downtime.

Your Briefcase—a Traveling Office

#191

*Be sure to carry a
well-stocked briefcase.*

There are all kinds of briefcases on the market. Find one with the proper number of compartments, pockets, and other features to suit your needs. Get a good one. Leather is best. Your briefcase should look professional and be a part of the total look you want to convey. Carry it with you in the car, on the airplane, or anywhere else you go. Keep the following items in your briefcase:

1. Your day planner. Keep only one calendar. Some people keep a desk calendar and a travel calendar. If you keep two calendars, you will forget to record appointments on one calendar or the other. You will end up missing meetings or key appointments because you will have scheduled them on one calendar but not on the other. If you have a secretary, it is a good idea for that person to be aware of your schedule—but have the secretary keep a separate calendar. The two of you should periodically review your schedules so that your secretary can update his or her calendar.

2. Post-it™ notes and a legal pad

3. Portable recording device

4. Mobile phone (optional)

5. Stamps, company stationery, and envelopes

6. Address and personal phone book (this may be part of your day planner)

7. Accessories (stapler and staples, paper clips, scissors, tape, rubber bands, ruler, pens and pencils with erasers, a highlighter pen, and a few file folders)

8. Laptop, notebook or tablet computer (optional)

> Your productivity will be greater if you carry these things with you when you travel because you won't have to spend time (and money) looking for them.

Traveling Effectively With Your Computer

#192

If you are computer-oriented, consider making the laptop (or computer notebook or powerbook) your constant traveling companion.

There are countless portable computers to choose from, and the list is growing every day. There is also a multitude of software programs available for them.

Follow these care and maintenance tips while traveling with your computer:

✓ Never check your computer with other luggage. Seasoned travelers know this, but if you are an occasional traveler, keep it in mind.

✓ Experts disagree on whether passing your PC through metal detectors will harm it. Play it safe. Send it through the X-ray conveyor belt.

✓ It is unlikely that CD or DVD discs will be harmed by X-ray machines; nonetheless, it is probably a good idea to remove the discs from your PC and have them checked by hand.

✓ One of the most important ways to protect information stored in a PC is to "park," or immobilize, the hard drive while traveling. Instructions provided with the computer will show you how to do this. Parking the hard drive keeps the PC's head—the device that actually reads or writes on a disk—from bouncing up and down and being damaged. Some PCs automatically park the hard disk when you turn it off. When you purchase a PC, check to see whether the PC you are purchasing has this feature.

✓ Beware of the common magnet! It can harm your PC. Keep disks away from handheld calculators, televisions, fluorescent lights, some telephones, and stereo speakers.

#193

Safeguard your computer while traveling.

Here are some additional considerations you should be aware of when traveling with a computer:

✓ **Arrive early.** You may be delayed if security personnel at the airport ask you to turn your computer on to be sure it is not a cleverly disguised bomb.

✓ **Carry-on limitations.** You can usually carry on no more than two pieces of luggage. Plan ahead.

✓ **Batteries.** The average battery for a laptop lasts about two hours. Carry extras, but realize they will add more weight.

✓ **Seat space.** If you normally travel first class, you will likely have plenty of room; however, most business people travel coach. Be careful. Your screen may fold up on your tray table if the person in front of you leans back.

Productivity for the Airline Traveler

Traveling to business appointments, or even on vacation trips, can be strenuous, stressful, and demanding. If you aren't careful and if you don't pace yourself, you can many times defeat the purpose of your business trip or vacation—to conduct business or to relax and enjoy yourself. Consider these tips:

#194

Get to the airport early.

If you think of your briefcase as a traveling office, you will have everything you need to conduct business, and you will alleviate the stress of running down the concourse at the last minute hoping you will catch your plane.

"It is better to wait a little while for your plane than to wait any time for the next one!"

Paul Heacock

#195

If you travel frequently, join an airline club that has facilities at your hometown airport.

All the major airlines have airline clubs. The club room is equipped with telephones, plush chairs, refreshments, fax machines, and often private rooms where you can conduct business meetings.

Be sure to pick a club that has a facility at your home airport so that when you get to the airport early, you have a place to go to work or relax. Also, the airline club you choose should have club facilities in the hub airports that you frequent most often.

#196

Choose an efficient travel agency.

Find one that truly provides outstanding service. This is extremely important. A good travel service will take a personal interest in you and book the most convenient flights at the best prices. The agency will seek out your travel preferences—your seat preferences, airplane and hotel preferences, and preferred room accommodations.

"Even if you're on the right track, you'll get run over if you just sit there."

Will Rogers

#197
Subscribe to an airline travel schedule guide.

These are scheduling booklets, updated at least monthly, of all flights to all travel destinations. These guides can be a lifesaver when you miss a flight or when one is cancelled or delayed. You can know in an instant what your options are for getting to your destination city. Rather than waiting in lines, you can go to the telephone (or use your mobile phone) to call the airline and change your flight.

#198
Be aware of the "best" seats on the aircraft.

Although it's really a matter of personal preference, most business people in the coach section prefer aisle seats, particularly on long flights. It is easier to get up and move around. However, if you like to look at the scenery, then a window seat is for you.

If you are tall or long-legged, the exit aisle on many airplanes has a little more leg room. If you are trying to work in cramped space, it can be very difficult to be productive. Seek out that extra room.

Once the plane takes off, look around if you aren't happy with your seat. Move if you can. On late-night flights, see if you can get your own row, usually three seats across. That way you can stretch out and rest, which may help you to be more productive the next day.

#199
Fly first class or business class when you can.

Flying first class rather than coach is the difference between a luxury car and a compact model. There's no comparison. You are treated much better, you have more room, and the food is better. It is quieter, and there is a good chance that the other people who are seated in this section will respect your privacy—because that's what they want too. Also, since you will be at the front of the plane, you will be among the first off and can get right to your appointments (if you don't need to wait for luggage). Although most businesses these days can't afford to let their employees fly first class, take advantage of it if you can.

Hint: Be sure to join all the frequent flyer clubs that award you free tickets and upgrades for the miles you travel. Most airlines have such clubs. You can use your mileage points to take vacations or to upgrade to first class.

More Tips for Traveling Effectively

#200

Travel with what you need.

Travelers are often advised to travel "light." Frequently, that is good advice. But be sure to take what you need to be comfortable. If you are away from home regularly, you probably want to bring some of the comforts of home with you. For example, if you are a walker or runner, bring the right shoes; bring your tea bags or instant coffee if you enjoy a frequent cup; carry a laptop computer if that's what you need.

Do try to carry no more than two bags, including your briefcase, so you can avoid checking your luggage. If you really want to be unproductive, try standing at the luggage carousel waiting on your luggage for 15 minutes to a half hour.

> *Travel hint:* Pack your suits and dresses in plastic bags (the kind you get from the cleaners) to keep your clothes from wrinkling. Be sure to store the plastic bags on a high shelf when you're not using them so that they aren't a safety hazard for children and pets.

> *"The world steps aside to let pass the people who know where they are going."*
>
> Anonymous

#201

If you rent cars when traveling, join car rental clubs.

Pick one or two car rental clubs and be a frequent renter. Many car rental companies now have procedures and benefits that save club members from having to wait in long lines when renting or returning a car.

#202

Schedule meetings at hotels or other facilities that are close to the airport you are traveling to.

Holding meetings in the airport's facilities can be a real timesaver. Most airport hotels have free courtesy transportation to and from the airport. You can be to your destination in a few minutes.

And don't forget about those airline clubs with meeting rooms. If there is one in the airport you are traveling to, you may be able to fly in, conduct business, and go home or to your next destination all in one day, without ever leaving the airport.

#203

Live life where you are.

When you travel into different time zones, promptly set your watch to the local time and begin adjusting to it immediately. Some people keep their watches on their home time. Their mind-set then is to think about what they would be doing at home rather than what they're doing in the present.

Example: If you live on the West Coast and travel to the East Coast, you may awaken at 6:00 a.m. Eastern time, but if your watch is still set for home, your mind-set is 3:00 a.m. Western time. The first thought that may go through your mind as you awaken is, "Boy am I going to be tired today." Avoid those negative mind-sets by living in the time zone where you are.

The following thoughts are gleaned from a review by Margaret Engel of Charles Kuralt's book *A Life on the Road* (Putnam.) The review appeared in the *Washington Post Book World*. Here is what Mr. Kuralt suggests to travelers:

"Never sleep on the side of the bed next to the telephone. (Everyone else does, destroying the mattress on that side). Travelers should carry a big safety pin (to pin room curtains that never meet), rubber sink stoppers (bad motel plumbing), and 100-watt bulbs.

Travelers should stay off the interstates (boring), ask for dry toast (or else face oozing grease), and save all the quarters they get in change for newspaper boxes, toll booths, and soft drink machines …

The traveler setting out without a pocketful of quarters in America today is (like) a soldier going into battle without ammo."

CHAPTER 18

How to Delegate for Greater Productivity

> "Don't do anything
> that someone else can
> do for you."
>
> Bill Marriott, Sr.

Delegation Basics

A *definition of delegation:* Getting things done through others while building their self-esteem and skill in the process.

How much is *not* delegating costing you and your organization? Each task should be done at the lowest economic level consistent with the quality required. People doing the jobs that employees paid less could do are robbing themselves of time, their people of development, and their organization of resources.

Example: If you are a middle manager typing your own letters, your secretary's skills are not being fully utilized.

Here are several benefits of delegation:

✓ Frees your time for other tasks

✓ Enriches and challenges other people

✓ Educates and trains other people

✓ May produce better results

✓ More cost effective

✓ Increases your span of accountability

> ### "None of us can do the job as well as all of us."
>
> (well-known saying)

In *The Creative Edge,* William C. Miller defines five levels of delegation:

1. **Tell:** "Based on my decision, here's what I want you to do."
2. **Sell:** "Based on my decision, here's what I want you to do because ... "
3. **Consult:** "Before I make a decision, I want your input."
4. **Participate:** "We need to make a decision together."
5. **Delegate:** "You make a decision."

Miller points out that delegation can be accomplished in three ways:

1. **Ask:** "Produce this result and ask me before you take any further action."
2. **Inform:** "Produce this result and keep me informed of what action you've taken."
3. **Do:** "Produce this result and I don't need to know what you have done."

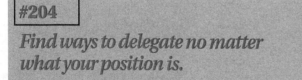

#204

Find ways to delegate no matter what your position is.

Some people don't think they are in a position to delegate because they have no formal authority. In fact, they perceive that everyone else delegates to them (or dumps on them). But even if you're at the bottom of the organization, it's possible for you to give some of your work to others. Become more productive by working as a team with co-workers. Instead of delegating, you are negotiating.

Example: "If you help me get this mailing out this evening, I'll help you with your phone calls tomorrow."

Be creative!

Find a way to delegate to co-workers so that you are not overwhelmed and headed for failure.

Why People Resist Delegating

Although we know it's important to delegate, sometimes we don't. Here's why:

- *"I can do it better."*
  We don't let go because we fear that the other person won't work with the same quality. In the beginning, you may be right. The other person may not have developed the particular skill as well as you have. But remember, that person never will if he or she isn't given the opportunity. Remember when your parents delegated the responsibility of driving to you? They may have felt uneasy about doing so. But you probably couldn't wait, although you may have felt awkward and afraid. You probably have great confidence now.

- *"It's easier to do it myself."*
  By the time you teach someone else and oversee their work, you could have finished the job yourself. That may actually be true. But if it's a recurring task, you'll always have to do it if you don't take the time to teach someone else.

- *"I don't trust them."*
  Lack of trust is one of the major reasons people don't delegate. You may recall that the last time you delegated a task to someone, you got burned. The person may have made mistakes that jeopardized the whole project.

The real questions to ask yourself are:

- Was the task properly delegated?

- Was it explained properly?

- Did the employee have the resources to carry out the task?

- Did the employee know what was trying to be achieved?

- Did you monitor the employee's progress and make him or her accountable?

- Did you provide direction?

Remember the procrastination quadrant on the Productivity Paradigm in Chapter 1. People may procrastinate or make mistakes if they have not been delegated the task properly.

> *"You will make mistakes, but make them with enthusiasm."*
>
> Colette

- *"No one can do the job as well as I can."* This is perfectionism. Remember that perfectionism is one of the primary reasons for procrastination. You take on too much work, but you don't let go of anything because you want the job done perfectly. The only problem is that you don't have enough time to do it all. And, if you don't delegate, you'll have to put something on hold.

- *"They might do the job better."* Not delegating because the other person may do the job better is related to your own lack of self-confidence. You don't delegate because you fear you will be shown up. You could even begin to think that you are replaceable. Guess what? We all are.

  Instead of holding others back, give them the opportunity to shine by delegating important work to them. If you do this, you may indeed be replaced—but only because you have been promoted. You will be recognized as one who "builds" others.

- *"I'll lose my power."* This reaction, too, may be related to a lack of self-confidence. You don't give up your authority or responsibility when you delegate. You just share it. You give others the opportunity to grow, and you relieve yourself of some of the pressure. It is true that those you delegate to may get promoted. But so will you, if you are seen as someone who helps others to grow. Plus you will be respected by those you help.

  Empower others by sharing your power. Then you will have real power—productivity power!

The Story About Four People: Everybody, Somebody, Anybody, and Nobody

There was an important job to be done and Everybody was asked to do it. Everybody was sure that Somebody would do it. Anybody could have done it, but Nobody did it. Somebody got angry about it because it was Everybody's job.

Everybody thought that Anybody could do it, and Nobody realized that Everybody wouldn't do it. It ended up that Everybody blamed Somebody when actually Nobody blamed Anybody.

Does this sound familiar to Anybody? Learn to clearly define who is to do what. Let go. DELEGATE.

"To get the full value of joy, you must have somebody to divide it with."

Mark Twain

When You Are the Delegator

#205

Clearly communicate when you delegate. Explain the task specifically and thoroughly.

Explain the details and ask for feedback to be sure the person you are delegating to understands the task.

Here is an example of what can happen when you don't communicate your delegated tasks clearly:

> A colonel gave the following order to his chief officer: "Tomorrow evening at approximately 1900 hours, Haley's Comet will appear in this area, an event that happens only once every 75 years. Have the troops fall in, in battalion area in fatigues, and I will give a talk on this rare phenomenon. If it rains, we will not be able to see it, so assemble the troops in the theatre and we will watch films of it."
>
> The chief officer went to the company commander and said: "The colonel has ordered that tomorrow at 1900 hours Haley's Comet will appear above the battalion area. If it rains, fall the troops in, in fatigues, and march to the theatre where the rare phenomenon will take place, something which occurs only once every 75 years."
>
> The company commander went to the lieutenant and said: "By order of the colonel in fatigues, at 1900 hours tomorrow evening the phenomenal Haley's Comet will appear in the theatre. In case of rain in the battalion area, the colonel will give another order, something which has happened only once every 75 years."
>
> The lieutenant, hearing this, gave the sergeant the following order: "Tomorrow at 1900 hours, the colonel will appear in the theatre with Haley's Comet, something which happens every 75 years. In case of rain, the colonel will order the comet into the battalion area."
>
> The sergeant went to the squad and said: "When it rains tomorrow at 1900 hours, the phenomenal 75-year-old colonel Haley will drive a Comet into the battalion area."

Message: Be sure that the message the delegatee receives is the same one you sent.

#206

Define the purpose.

Communicate what you are trying to achieve as an end result. Show the person you are delegating to "the picture on the box." (See Idea #52.)

#207

Communicate what's in it for the delegatee.

Will the person learn a new skill? Get to meet new people? Earn more money? Gain visibility? Possibly be promoted? Have fun? Be challenged? A delegatee who sees some benefit is more likely to be committed to the task.

#208

Give and get feedback about how to do the task.

Provide direction by practicing Management By Walking Around. Help delegates succeed. Be accessible so that they can give you feedback.

#209

Give the delegatee authority and responsibility.

Many times a delegatee is given responsibility, but no authority to make decisions. Think about it from your perspective. Have you ever been delegated a task but not been given authority to make any decisions? It's frustrating. The message the delegatee sometimes perceives is "You want me to be responsible for getting the work done, but you don't trust me to make decisions."

#210

Don't hover.

Really give the job away. It's frustrating to the delegatee to be stood over and watched. Give the person some breathing space.

"Seagulling" is another term for hovering: The manager flies in unannounced, makes a big flap, and dumps on people. It doesn't help to hover. It puts employees on edge and makes them feel like you don't trust them.

#211

Delegate methodology.

This is extremely important. Allow others to do a task their way. They are more likely to take ownership. But use common sense. If you are working with a new employee, you may decide not to give that person as much freedom as you would a more experienced person. Review the levels of delegation discussed earlier in this chapter.

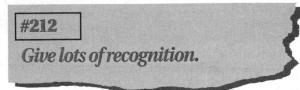

#212

Give lots of recognition.

Praise people as they are carrying out the work that was delegated to them. This helps build their self-confidence and also creates a positive relationship. Michael LeBoeuf wrote a book called *The Greatest Management Principle in the World* (Putnam, 1985). He believes that the greatest management principle is that people will do what they are rewarded for. Reward or recognize people for good performance. If you do, they will likely strive for excellence again and again. Be sure that your praise is sincere.

#213

Make the delegatee accountable: establish interim deadlines for accomplishments.

Don't make the mistake of totally giving away the job and assuming that it will get done. Set up interim "report back" dates to formally discuss progress and problems.

#214

Give positive and corrective feedback.

Idea #208 suggested giving delegatees feedback about the tasks they are doing. It is equally important to concentrate on the people doing the tasks. Let them know where they stand and how they are doing.

Here are some examples of both positive and corrective feedback:

Positive feedback	**Corrective feedback**
Concentrate on what the person did well and the behavior you want to see repeated. Be specific. It probably isn't good enough to say "good job," although that's better than saying nothing.	Concentrate on the behavior you want to see changed. What does the individual need to do differently? The emphasis is on the behavior, not the person.
Example: "John, thanks for getting that report in on time. It was brief, concise, to the point, and had logical conclusions. I appreciate it. Good job!"	*Example:* "Elaine, I've noticed that the productivity reports have been consistently late. I'd appreciate knowing what will help you get them in on time. It's important that we adhere to the deadlines."
Now John knows what is important—turning in on time a report that is brief, concise, to the point and has valid conclusions. He knows what to do and how to act next time.	

When You Are the Delegatee

When work is being delegated to you fast and furiously, be in control as you are accepting it. Ask yourself, "What do I need to know to be more productive in this situation?"

"Carry a cat by the tail and you will learn things you won't learn any other way."

Mark Twain

Here are some ways for staying in control:

#215

Ask for the resources.

If the person delegating to you isn't clear and specific about what resources you will be given to get the job done, ask for them. Specifically, you will want to know:

- How much time you will have.

- What human resources you will be given.

- Your budget.

- What material resources you will receive (supplies, inventory, tools, etc.).

Remember, if you don't ask, you probably won't receive any more than you were given (which may not be enough). To gain control over the task, ask for what you need and document why you need it. Review the section on negotiating in Chapter 15.

#216

Seek out authority.

If it hasn't been given to you, ask for it up front. Sometimes supervisors forget to formally give authority. If you don't get it right from the start, you could be set up. For instance, if you make a decision the delegator disagrees with, he or she may say, "Who gave you the authority?"

If you are supervising others or if you are working on a project with several other people and you have been delegated the responsibility of being in charge, be sure that the delegator makes it official. He or she should document in writing that you are in charge, that you have the authority to provide direction and guidance, and that you have the authority to assist in making decisions and solving problems.

#217

Make yourself accountable.

Schedule regular meetings with the delegator to give and get feedback. Let the delegator know that you want to be accountable.

Sometimes delegatees think they can breathe easier if no one makes them accountable. Their thinking is: "No one made me accountable, so no one will know or care if I mess up."

Is that a good way to go into a project or task? Absolutely not. You are, in effect, programming yourself for failure. Look at it from the other perspective—plan to be successful. Make it clear that you want the delegator and others to know what you are doing. One of the biggest complaints people have is that they don't get any recognition. Wave your success under your supervisor's nose. You don't have to flaunt it, but you need to get management's attention.

#218

Find out what potential traps exist.

It's helpful to have a little past experience (if there is some) to avoid making the same mistakes others have made. You can be more productive if you can avoid the pitfalls of the past.

#219

Say no assertively to new tasks when you are overloaded.

Here's how you can do it using the USA method:

Understanding statement: "I know that this is an important job."

Situation: "I'm really busy with the tasks and projects I have presently."

Action statement: "I would prefer not to overload myself. If I do, I won't be able to do this job with the quality I know you expect."

Keep this in mind: If you don't speak up, nothing will change. You will continue to get dumped on. Furthermore, you will inadvertently train other people that it is all right to give you more work whenever they feel like it.

CHAPTER 19

Stress and Burnout: Pacing Yourself for Greater Productivity

> *"Your success and happiness lie in you ... Resolve to keep happy, and your joy and you shall form an invincible host against difficulties."*
>
> Helen Keller

What Is Stress?

Stress is good! Yes, that's right. Up to a point. It becomes a problem only when it starts to control us. The late Dr. Hans Selye, a pioneer in stress research, said that we need to find our personal best stress level. Some people are naturally racehorses. Others are more "turtle-like." They move at a slower pace. When these people are beset with conditions that are different from what they are used to, they may feel out of control and stressful.

Chapter 7 discussed dealing with on-the-job crises and turtles who find themselves in racehorse jobs. These people are better off finding a line of work that is more in agreement with who they are. Try to make your job fit the kind of person you are.

Here is Dr. Selye's definition of stress:

Stress is the nonspecific response of the body to any demand made upon it, or the rate of wear and tear on the body caused by living. (What counts is how we handle those demands. It's important to be in control.)

Another good definition is that stress is a perception of threat or an expectation of future discomfort that arouses, alerts, or otherwise activates the organism.

Think about that: *"perception of threat"* or *"expectation of future discomfort."* What does that mean?

Consider this example:

Do you like to fly? If you answered no, you're not alone. How do you feel when you get on the airplane? Perhaps tense or nauseated. Your heart may begin to race, you may feel warm, your forehead may begin to perspire, your palms may grow sweaty, your breathing may become rapid, or you may hold the arms of your seat tightly. In short, you may be a white-knuckle flier.

If so, you are experiencing the stress response. Your body has a perception of threat and an expectation of future discomfort. It's going to hurt when that plane crashes!

But if you like to fly, you have a different perception. You don't see a threat or an expectation of future discomfort. You see pleasure and relaxation. You might think to yourself: "There are no phones up here I must answer. No one will interrupt me. I can read, study, write, or rest. It's my choice. This feels great."

As you can see, there can be two people on the same airplane going to the same destination but each with a different perception of the outcome. Stress, then, is personal. What is a perception of threat and an expectation of future discomfort to one person may be a pleasurable experience to another.

Stress and How It Relates to Burnout

The stress response, as mentioned previously, is what Dr. Walter Cannon calls the reaction we have when we are under stress. It is a result of the "fight or flight" syndrome.

We human beings were made to protect ourselves. Thousands of years ago we had to fight off or flee from our predators. Our brains sent signals to make certain organs and glands secrete chemicals such as adrenaline to help us fight or flee. Our heart rate increased, our vision became more acute, our bodies tensed up for the fight. We grew warm with the more intense flow of blood. We were prepared to fight or flee.

We still react the same way today, although our predators are no longer saber-toothed tigers.

Instead they are our co-workers, bosses, employees, customers, spouses, children, the traffic, long lines, and too much work. We prepare ourselves to fight or flee.

If you perceive most life events as stressful (a perception of threat or future discomfort) you are likely to be in a somewhat constant state of readiness to fight or flee. As a result, your body is constantly preparing itself. Pretty soon, your blood pressure begins to stay elevated, you are continually tense, you have difficulty sleeping, and you begin to lash out at others or retreat into privacy (fight or flee). Over a period of time, this stress takes a toll on you physically and mentally. You get tired of fighting back. This is called burnout.

- Burnout is physical or emotional exhaustion caused by excessive demands on emotions, energy, and other resources.

- Burnout occurs when a person works too hard for too long or endures too many stressors over a short period of time.

"The trouble with the rat race is even if you win, you're still a rat."

Lily Tomlin

Dealing With Stress: How to Get Control

The key to managing stress is knowing what it is that causes your stress.

Remember, different things cause stress for different people. If you can identify your stressors, you can begin to change your behavior.

Some people let their stressors get the best of them. These people burn out and may have severe physical or mental problems as a result.

#221

Always look at the options you have for overcoming a stressor, and change your behavior to overcome it.

Unfortunately, you can be so close to your stressful situation, such as a difficult job or relationship, that you "can't see the forest for the trees." In these situations, get someone else to help you explore your options.

#222

Seek out personal support systems.

Personal support system is a fancy term for "friends." Who can you talk to when you are under stress? Some people just hold it in. Develop a good support network.

#223

Get counseling if you need it.

A more formal support system is counseling. Seek out a qualified professional if your life stressors are complex and difficult. Unfortunately, our society still causes us to think that seeking professional counseling is a sign of weakness. The message is this: If you can't handle the stress, you're a weakling.

But guess what? There are a lot of weaklings out there. One out of three Americans seriously thought about quitting their jobs in 1990 because of workplace stress. According to a survey by Northwestern National Life Insurance Company, seven of 10 workers stated that stress caused frequent health problems and made them less productive. 53 percent said they were required to work more than 40 hours a week very often or somewhat often.

If you are really hurting, job-related or otherwise, don't let the social stigma of counseling stop you from getting help.

Coping with a stressor

If you don't like to fly on airplanes, what is your recourse? How can you change your behavior? First, look at your options.

- Can you reasonably drive to your destination? (If it is across the state, perhaps so. If it is across the country, then it's probably not a reasonable option.)
- If you must fly, perhaps you can take a good book and focus your attention on it.
- Practice controlling your body—try deep-breathing exercises and relaxation. This is not always easy to do, but it can help.
- Learn a little about aerodynamics. Why does an airplane stay in the air? What are the odds that something will happen?
- Do you have to go at all? Perhaps you can stay home.

Choose the options that seem viable. If none of them seem so to you, then what alternatives can you think of?

If your job requires you to fly often, perhaps you can transfer to another department where there isn't as much travel.

The point of this example is that you must identify what causes your stress and then change your behavior to deal with it effectively.

Changing Your Behavior

Chapter 9 discussed how you could change your behavior to achieve greater productivity.
Here's an example of how that relates to life stressors:

Awareness

> Standing in grocery store lines on Saturday morning drives you crazy. You jump up and down, you grow tense and angry, and you say to yourself, "Why do I put myself through this?" Then you discover that there are options. Maybe you don't need to tolerate these conditions.

Commitment

> You tell yourself that you will shop on Saturday mornings between the hours of 7:00 and 9:00 only, before most shoppers are up. That way, you won't have to stand in lines. Of course, you must change your behavior to get up on Saturday morning to beat the crowd.

Discipline

> On Saturday morning, your alarm clock goes off at 6:30. You are tempted to stay in bed. However, you discipline yourself to get up and go to the store. You whiz through the store and the checkout counter and you are home by 8:30 a.m. You can now enjoy the rest of the day and the peace and quiet of a beautiful Saturday morning.

Remember that you always have options to stressors. It is when people feel that they have no options that they begin to burn out. They lose hope and give up. Don't let that happen to you.

#224

Don't try to change everything or too many things at the same time.

Consider that change itself is stressful. Don't set yourself up for failure. Choose carefully and wisely what you want to change and keep in mind that how well you control life's stressors has a great deal to do with how productive you are.

"If one advances confidently in the direction of his dreams, and endeavors to live the life he has imagined, he will meet with a success unexpected ..."

Henry David Thoreau

Dealing With Stress at Work

Stress in the workplace is a major contributor to decreased productivity. Health problems caused by stress, rather than physical illness, are taking a substantial toll in worker absenteeism, according to the results of a Louis Harris survey reported in the *Wall Street Journal*. A quarter of those interviewed said they had stress-linked problems and half of those people said the problems restricted their routine. The median for days disabled: 18 a year.

Studies that link decreased productivity to work-related stress abound. How can you avoid stress? You can't. What you can do is deal with it.

How can you deal with it effectively? By following all the advice in this book. Consider how the ideas in this book can be linked to the following survey responses. When asked what factors caused the most stress on the job, surveyed workers said:*

Not doing the kind of work I want to

34%

Set a goal to find a job or start a business that you can enjoy and one that you can prosper in.

Coping with current job

30%

Set goals, plan, schedule activities, prioritize, work in time blocks and on only one thing at a time. Get control of daily obstacles, and clearly communicate all the things you've been reading about in this book.

Working too hard

28%

Limit your hours—the work will still be there tomorrow. It always will be. Work on the right things. Be sure to do some high-payoff work everyday. Take breaks. Talk with those in your personal support system.

Colleagues at work

21%

Communicate with your colleagues. Stay calm with the difficult ones. Document activities and follow up with those who don't follow through. Reward those who do a good job and who assist you. They will reward you back. You get what you give.

A difficult boss

18%

Communicate to try to resolve differences. If that doesn't work, look for a new job. Life is too short to be around difficult people for eight hours a day.

*Respondents could list more than one factor.

Source: D'Arcy Masius Benton and Bowles, Inc.
Fears and Fantasies of the American Consumer. May, 1986.

Four Ways Managers Create a Stress-ridden Environment

- **Exhibit unpredictable behavior.** One day your supervisor is "up" and positive and helpful. The next day he or she is "down" and wants to "beat everybody up."

- **Whittle away at employees' self-esteem.** These are the put downs and accusations that put people on edge, make them fearful of losing their jobs, and cause them to lose confidence.

- **Create win-lose situations.** The idea of creating unhealthy competition between employees and departments, causing them to withhold information and become suspicious of each other.

- **Understimulate or overstimulate employees.** This is called "rustout" (boredom) or "burnout" (overwhelmed and overextended). Either extreme can be stressful.

*Source: Kenneth Blanchard, "Management Malpractice—
Five Ways to Avoid Giving Your Employer Ulcers,"
Success Magazine (September 1986).

At a joint meeting of the National Institute for Occupational Safety and Health and the American Psychological Association, these statistics and facts were presented:

- Job stress siphons between $100 billion and $300 billion a year from the U.S. economy.

- Job stress contributes to fatigue, high blood pressure, and heart attacks.

- Workers under stress are more prone to drink too much, eat too much, and exercise too little.

- Job stress carries into the home.

- High job stress and low job satisfaction greatly increase a worker's likelihood of having burning eyes, rashes, headaches, nasal problems, and sore throats. It also contributes to increased irritability, drowsiness, lethargy, and nervousness that are only experienced at the work site.

"We all surrender some part of our personality to the organization … The important thing is not so much the organization's pressures as the need to be aware of them. What's devastating is the number of people who find organization ideas superior to their own. They surrender and they enjoy it."

John Kenneth Galbraith

How to Avoid Creating A Stressful Climate

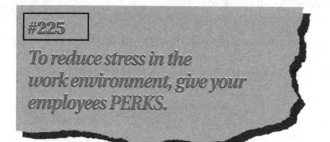

#225

To reduce stress in the work environment, give your employees PERKS.

"More men are killed by overwork than the importance of the world justifies."

Rudyard Kipling

Dr. Kenneth Blanchard, of *One-Minute Manager* fame, suggests these perks:

Participation. Allow people to participate in their own outcomes. They feel in control of their own destiny and have the opportunity to use their knowledge.

Environment. Climate is what people feel and experience as they work in your organization. Strive to create a climate that is warm and friendly, one in which people are treated with dignity and respect and as part of the company family. If employees like what they feel and experience, they are apt to stay. If not, they are likely to move on.

Recognition. Give it to people for their hard work and accomplishments! Doing so speaks for itself.

Knowledge. Help people get the training and information they need to do their jobs and give them the opportunity to share and use what they already know. Send them to seminars, and conduct on-site training sessions. When people don't know how to do their jobs, it creates stress not only for them but for everyone who works with them. The bottom line is decreased productivity.

> *Comment:* One of the biggest problems in business today is that employees aren't being well-trained. Many organizations just give lip service to it. In fact, when companies experience an economic downturn, what is one of the first things to go? Training. Just when people need it the most. During these times, in particular, they need training on how to be productive and how to work as a team because often they will be expected to do more with less. People put in more hours, but they don't know how to work efficiently or with each other. They burn out and they leave. The company must then replace them. This turnover actually forces the company to spend more money on lost productivity than it would have spent on training and providing employees with job knowledge.

Style. Follow a consistent management style. Be predictable. Let people feel safe approaching you. Encourage them to be open with you and to really communicate with you.

All of these ideas apply particularly to supervisors, but they are just as valid for employees and co-workers. They also work effectively with your spouse, friends, and children.

Managing Stress Day by Day

#226

Work on only one thing at a time.

Here's what can happen: You come to work with your "To Do" list in hand. You sit down at your desk, which is piled high with mail. Hastily, you begin to sort through it, holding your "To Do" list in abeyance. About that time, the telephone rings. Almost subconsciously, you answer it. At the same time, you continue opening your mail and try to read it. Now, your supervisor sees you, walks toward you, and whispers loudly, "I need to see you as soon as you get off the phone." You acknowledge her by nodding your head. At this moment you are: (1) trying to pay attention to your "To Do" list, (2) talking on the phone, (3) listening to the person on the phone, (4) opening your mail, and (5) acknowledging your supervisor. But, what are you actually accomplishing? NOTHING. Because you are trying to do *five* things at once. It isn't possible. The key is concentration—devoting your full attention to one task and bringing it to closure (finish) or to a convenient stopping point so that you can work on something else.

#227

Nurture relationships.

Good mental health and productivity depend on having people around to talk with, to share successes and failures with, to vent frustrations with, to laugh and cry with, and to play and work with.

"I am still determined to be cheerful and to be happy in whatever situation I may be, for I have also learned from experience that the greater part of our happiness or misery depends upon our dispositions and not upon our circumstances."

Martha Washington

#228

Don't procrastinate. It causes stress.

The great legendary coach of the University of Alabama, the late Paul "Bear" Bryant, reportedly kept a sign in his locker room that said, "Cause something to happen." You can't do that if you put off taking action.

In his book *Beware the Naked Man Who Offers You His Shirt* (New York: William Morrow and Co., Inc., 1990), Harvey Mackey discusses failure and puts it into perspective. He writes: "Over 95 percent of Publishers-Clearinghouse Mailings get tossed. Yet by closing on only 1 out of every 25 prospects, it has set the standard for the industry …

When Lou Holtz was coaching at Minnesota, we had the most successful telephone drive selling season tickets in the school's history. We sold 6,000 tickets and it was a big item in the media. What we didn't tell the world was that we had to make 75,000 phone calls to do it."

Then he made a statement in the book that you should memorize and remember the next time you begin to procrastinate because you fear failure.

He said: *"Measure success by success, not by the number of failures it takes to achieve it."*

Remember, failure is just a process of becoming.

Instead have a "bias for action." That term comes from the book *In Search of Excellence*. The author points out that in excellent companies, management and employees have a bias to take action, to get things done, to be productive, and to get results.

There are three consequences of taking action:

1. **Success.** You follow through and complete the job with quality. Remember the definition of success:

$$\text{SUCCESS} = \frac{\text{DEFINED ACTIVITIES} \quad X \quad \text{DIRECTED ACTION} \quad X \quad \text{TIME ALLOCATED}}{\text{ANTICIPATED RESULTS (STANDARDS)}}$$

   Success, then, is completing with quality all the tasks to achieve a goal or finish a project.

2. **Remaining the same.** You take action, but nothing *seems* to change. Note the word *seems*. At the very least, if you take action, you are learning, so something is changing—your knowledge level.

   Sometimes, however, people don't seem to make progress, so they put off the job in favor of something else that is easier or that gives them immediate results. But in the back of their mind they are thinking about the task they are putting off. It becomes more stressful than following through.

3. **Failure.** The fear of failure is immobilizing. To overcome the fear of failure, first change your mind-set. See yourself being able to accomplish the task. Second, commit to action by listing the activity on your "To Do" list, and then transfer it to your daily plan.

> *"How would you like it when every time you make a mistake a big red light goes on and 18,000 people boo?"*
>
> Jacques Plante (former hockey goalie)

#229

Fight only for the things that are really worth it. Don't sweat the small stuff.

This is called prioritizing. Consider what your real priorities are at work and at home. They are the goals, objectives, and activities that give you the greatest payoff.

Yet, particularly at work, we tend to think that everything is important. Other people even tell us that. If you ask, "What's really important for us to accomplish today?" you may very well hear, "Everything." Well, "everything" may need to get done, but the real question is what must get done in the hours that you have available to accomplish something meaningful.

So:

Rule #1: Don't sweat the small stuff.

Rule #2: It's all small stuff.

Rule #3: If you can't fight and you can't flee, flow.

Obviously, not everything in your life is small stuff. But this facetious little phrase helps put life's tasks into perspective. What is really important? Think about your real payoffs in life. Are you pursuing them?

"A perfectionist is someone who takes great pains in everything he or she does and gives them to everyone else."

Anonymous

#230

Reject perfectionism.

Perfectionism behavior is procrastination behavior and, thus, is stressful. The perfectionist doesn't have a bias for action. The perfectionist has a bias for correction. The question should be "When will we implement?" The question the perfectionist continually asks is "How can I make this better?" Perfectionists forget about deadlines and the needs of others. Their focus of attention is that their work must be so perfect that no one can criticize it.

Of course, it doesn't matter how "perfect" their work is because there will always be others who don't think it is. Perfectionists, then, grow frustrated because others don't see their work as perfect and because deadlines creep up on them and put pressure on them to complete the job. Then they think, "We're running out of time, but it's not perfect yet."

If you add to this that perfectionists don't delegate because no one else can do the job well enough or up to their standards, you can see how being a perfectionist actually undermines productivity.

Charles Garfield, Ph.D., recorded an audio program a few years ago titled *Peak Performers* (Chicago: Nightingale Conant Corp.). Dr. Garfield conducted more than 1,500 in-depth interviews with top achievers to identify their common traits. He isolated specific behaviors that he believes enable top achievers to excel consistently. Many of those traits are related to skills outlined in this book—skills such as a strong sense of mission, goal setting, and planning. One trait peak performers share is the ability to reject perfectionism. They take action. They do a job well, but not perfectly.

Do you ever sit down after dinner to read the newspaper and say to yourself, "O.K. I'm going to relax now"? But then as you're sitting there trying to read the newspaper, a little voice goes off in the back of your mind that says: "I'm not going to let you relax today. You didn't finish all of your work today. You should be doing it right now. And if you're not going to do that work, then you should be washing dishes or cutting the grass or playing with the children or cleaning the house or something else meaningful rather than sitting here wasting your time."

What's going on here is the Puritan work ethic to the extreme. Yes, work is important, but so is learning how to relax. Learn to silence that little voice occasionally. Relaxation is vital to recharge your batteries so that when it is time to work, you can be productive.

#231
Learn to truly relax.

If you are trying to relax, but you are thinking about what you should be doing, then you are not relaxing.

Dr. Herbert Benson, of the University of Harvard Medical School, said it is necessary to learn how to relax to combat the effects of stress. He said that if there is a stress response, then there must also be a relaxation response. Learning to truly relax takes practice. Practice real relaxation for at least 20 to 30 minutes every day.

The ideal time is right when you get home from work. This relaxation period can serve as a transition from your workday to your personal day. If you really relax, you can re-energize yourself so that you can approach your personal day with vigor and enthusiasm instead of feeling worn out from work.

Of course, not everyone has the luxury of relaxing for 20 to 30 minutes after work. There is dinner to prepare, children to care for, household chores to do, meetings to attend, and other activities.

But do find a time to relax sometime during your busy day. If you don't, you may feel constantly fatigued.

> **To put it into perspective: Relaxation is the ability to do absolutely nothing and feel good about it.**

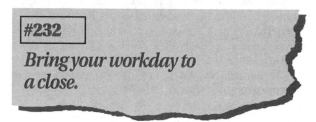

#232
Bring your workday to a close.

Get closure. Before you leave the office, your car, the plant, or wherever it is that you work, physically check off your accomplishments on your day planner. If you don't feel that you accomplished anything on a given day, don't "beat yourself up." Instead, vow to get it done tomorrow. Outline your daily plan for tomorrow. Then set your workday aside and focus your attention on your personal life. Put the workday out of your mind.

"Learn to pause ... or nothing worthwhile will catch up to you."

Doug King

#233

Leave your job tasks at work.

This is sometimes easier said than done, but practice putting work thoughts out of your mind as they enter your head. Consciously tell yourself, "I'm not going to think about this now." Tell yourself over and over again, if necessary.

If you bring work home occasionally or if you work out of your home, be sure to work in time blocks so that you don't become obsessive and consumed by the work. For example, resolve to work on your budget report between 7:00 p.m. and 9:00 p.m., and then list it on your day planner.

#234

Listen to your body.

When you are under stress, your body speaks to you because it goes into the fight or flight mode. Listen to what it is saying. It may be telling you that you are out of control and expending valuable energy on trivial or minor pursuits (spinning your wheels). Stop and review your daily plan. Put yourself back on course for productivity and accomplishment.

Think of yourself as a pilot who must navigate to keep the plane on course. If you are flying to Hawaii, you will need to be aware of your progress and chart your course. You will need to regularly assess whether you are still going in the right direction. Remember, if you follow a straight course you'll use less fuel—that is, less time and energy.

If you don't chart your progress and just assume that you are on target, you may run out of fuel before you get to Hawaii and "crash and burn."

You see the analogy. Be your own navigator. Use your energy wisely. Constantly monitor yourself so that you don't "crash and burn." (See Idea #48 in Chapter 7.)

The "One-minute Countdown" for Relaxation

If you are tense, uptight, and going "a hundred miles an hour" but getting nowhere during your day, consider this one-minute countdown for getting control of yourself.

Find a quiet place—your office (if you have one), the bathroom, your car, a conference room, or any quiet place where you won't be interrupted.

Sit down and tense your whole body from head to toe. Hold it for 20 seconds. Then release all the tension. Feel it leave your body.

Concentrate on your breathing. Breathe from your diaphragm. Close your eyes and sit back. See the number 4 in your mind. As you take a deep breath, see the 4 come towards you. As you exhale, see the 4 fade away.

Now picture a 3. See it come towards you as you take a deep breath. As you exhale, watch it fade away. Do the same thing with the numbers 2 and 1.

This process will take you about one minute. The idea is to get you to concentrate on your body, to refocus and to put yourself back in touch with your daily plan.

If you have more than a couple of minutes, use that time to sit and truly relax.

#235

Learn how to sleep effectively.

When people are stressful, they either can't sleep or don't reach the "deep sleep" stage or the REM (rapid eye movement) stage where true revitalization can occur.

When you go to bed at night, learn to put everything out of your mind or focus on something pleasant. If a worry enters your mind, consciously remove it. Tell yourself, "I am not going to think about this now because there is nothing I can do about it right now."

This process, named "thought stopping" by Duke University medical researcher Dr. Redford Williams, will take time to learn, but once you do, you will be pleasantly surprised at how much better you sleep.

Try this "thought stopping" exercise to remove unwanted thoughts:

Visualize a trash can. Remove the lid and drop the thought in the can and put the lid back on. If the thought tries to ooze out of the can, picture yourself sitting down on the can.

This tip may not work for everyone, but if you try it over a period of time, you will learn how to put unwanted thoughts out of your mind.

"The best cure for insomnia is to get a lot of sleep."

W.C. Fields

#236

Try "speed sleeping."

Speed sleeping? Sounds pretty crazy, right? Actually it's a term for describing "catnaps," those brief 15- to 30-minute naps that can reenergize and revitalize you. Catnaps are not the same as the "Saturday afternoon nap."

If you speed sleep, you awaken with renewed energy. If you take a two-hour nap on a Saturday afternoon in front of the TV, you probably feel like you've been hit in the head with a hammer when you wake up. This type of sleeping is "hammer sleeping." Here are the differences between "speed sleeping" and "hammer sleeping":

Speed Sleeping	Hammer Sleeping
15 to 30 minutes	Lengthy sleep, probably at least an hour
Reach the "alpha" stage of sleep—very light sleep	Reach the "delta" or "theta" stage of sleep—deep sleep—from which it is hard to awaken
Aware of your surroundings; may hear sounds and sense movement	Unaware of surroundings—sleep soundly
Awaken at your "programmed time" on your own	Someone probably needs to shake you to wake you up

Learning to speed sleep is an art. It is actually an extension of the relaxation response discussed earlier. Practice it. You probably won't get immediate results. But if you are committed to learning how to speed sleep, you can become quite proficient at it.

Programming yourself

Have you ever traveled out of town for an important meeting you had to attend at 8:00 the next morning?

The night before, when you set the alarm clock for 6:00 a.m., you thought, "Hey, how do I know that clock works?"

So you took out your travel alarm and set it for 6:00 a.m. Then you turned off the lights and headed for dreamland. But then you thought: "Wait a minute. I haven't used that travel alarm in a while. I'm not sure it still works."

To be safe, you called the front desk and left a wake-up call for 6:00 a.m. Satisfied that you had prepared for the worst-case scenario, you finally really went to bed.

What happened about 5:55 the next morning? You awakened because you programmed your subconscious mind to do so the night before.

Keep in mind that you have a remarkable ability for programming yourself to sleep effectively.

More Ideas to Manage Stress

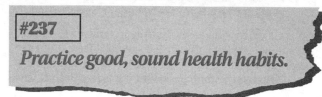

#237

Practice good, sound health habits.

Your mother was right when she told you to get plenty of rest, to eat right, and to take care of yourself. Life today is extremely demanding and requires you to be at your best.

Here are some health tips for leading a more productive life:

✓ **Find the right amount of sleep for you.** Each person requires a different amount of sleep. Some require eight hours of sleep a night, others only six or seven hours. Experiment with what is right for you. For example, if you currently get eight hours of sleep each night, try setting your alarm clock to awaken you 15 minutes earlier. Note how you feel after a few days. If you are bright and alert, you've just given yourself 15 minutes more a day for greater productivity. Conversely, if you're only getting six hours of sleep and are groggy, go to bed earlier. See how well you function on seven hours of sleep.

✓ **Eat right.** You don't have to be a nutritionist to know that there are some things that will get you into trouble nutritionally—too much caffeine, junk food (high sugar and fat content), and overeating or undereating. People who are under stress have a tendency to either gorge themselves or skip meals because they don't feel they have time to eat.

✓ **Exercise.** Exercise is one of the best ways to relieve tension and stress. Over a period of time, after you get into shape, you are likely to feel the energizing effects of exercise. You will probably feel more alert and be more productive.

Kinds of exercise

Isotonic
Rhythmic, repetitive exercise that involves motion. Isotonic exercise can be either aerobic or anaerobic.

Aerobic
Exercise that is continuous for 15 or more minutes (jogging, walking, swimming).

Anaerobic
Exercise of short duration, stop-and-go in rhythm, and low intensity in effort (golf or tennis).

Isometric
Exercise with very little movement such as lifting or pushing against a stationary object. Isometric exercise can improve muscle tone and can make you stronger. However, it doesn't improve your heart conditioning and may even be dangerous for heart patients.

Use common sense though. Many times, weekend athletes do themselves more harm than good. If you haven't been in the habit of exercising, have a physical examination first. Then go slow and easy and be consistent. Set a goal to do some kind of specific exercise (walking, jogging, swimming) at least three times a week for at least 15 minutes. Commit yourself to an exercise habit.

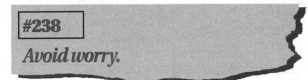

#238

Avoid worry.

That's kind of like telling someone to avoid sweets—easier said than done, but necessary. When you go to bed at night, or even in the middle of the day, push those worry thoughts out of your mind and replace them with productive thoughts. It requires practice, but it can, of course, be highly beneficial and productive. Use the following acronym to remember to avoid worry:

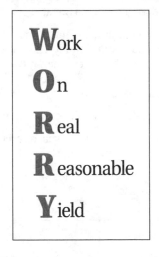

Work

On

Real

Reasonable

Yield

Worry thoughts are not real. They are the "what ifs" we imagine. What if I get into a car accident? What if I lose my job? What if my son or daughter gets sick? These are unproductive thoughts. The odds that these things will happen are minimal. The next time you find yourself worrying about the "what ifs," catch yourself and say, "I am going to put this out of my mind and work on something that is real and reasonable that will yield something that is productive."

To put "worry" into perspective, consider the following excerpt from an essay by Ralph Schoenstein that appeared in *The New Yorker*:

What a list! Something old and something new, something cosmic yet something trivial too, for the creative worrier must forever blend the pedestrian with the immemorial. If the sun burns out, will the Mets be able to play their entire schedule at night? If cryogenically frozen human beings are ever revived, will they have to register to vote? And if the little toe disappears, will field goals play a smaller part in the National Football League?

Funnel your worry thoughts into something productive.

Only about 2 percent of the average person's worrying time is spent on anything that might be helped or somehow improved by worrying. The other 98 percent of the time is spent (or wasted) as follows:

- **40%** on things that never happen

- **35%** on things that can't be changed

- **15%** on things that turn out better than expected

- **8%** on useless, petty worries

An important conclusion of this survey is that it's useless to worry about the trivial and about things that are unlikely to happen. It is important to put worry thoughts out of your mind and to replace them with productive thoughts.

Source: *The Office Professional.*
Professional Training Associates, Inc.
Round Rock, TX. 155N 0739-3156.

#239

Confront your irrational anger and hostility.

Do you ever lie in bed at night thinking about that "so-and-so" at work and how you will get him back? In your mind, you devise an elaborate scheme that you really won't ever implement. You get yourself all worked up and play out the scenario over and over in your mind, delaying precious rest. And while you are fretting, guess what that "so-and-so" is doing? Sleeping. He couldn't care less at that moment. Put negative and hostile thoughts out of your mind.

Pent-up hostility and anger can be a "killer." Find a proper way to release it. Develop a personal support system. These are the people who support you, the people you can talk to and vent your frustrations with. If you hold it all in, sooner or later, you're going to explode. When you do, it may be at an inappropriate time and place and with the wrong person. Release your anger by venting to your support systems.

Dr. Redford Williams, the medical researcher at Duke University who coined the term "thought stopping," wrote a book called *The Trusting Heart.* Although his research is continuing, his hypothesis is that there is a correlation between heart disease and pent-up frustration. This seems to be similar to the relationship between heart disease and Type A behavior.

Dr. Williams suggests, of course, that this hostility or anger should be released or set aside. His term thought stopping refers to the idea of pushing hostile thoughts out of the mind. He believes that people can train themselves to replace

hostile thoughts with pleasant ones, to confront irrational anger and set it aside, to think about something productive instead.

There's a story of a swami and a cobra who lived near a temple in Bengal. As people went in to worship, the cobra would bite them. Many people grew fearful and refused to visit the temple. The swami, who was master of the temple, called the cobra to him and, by means of a spell, made the snake promise he would never bite anyone again. Soon it became known that the snake had lost its venom and was no longer a threat.

People grew unafraid of the cobra, and boys began to tease the snake unmercifully. They hit it and dragged it across the stones. One day the temple swami summoned the snake to see if he had kept his promise. The snake was bruised and bleeding.

"How did this come to be?" asked the swami.

"I have been abused," said the snake, "ever since you condemned me to my promise."

"I told you not to bite," said the swami, "but I did not tell you not to hiss."

■ ■ ■

"I've had a few arguments with people, but I never carry a grudge. You know why? While you're carrying a grudge, they're out dancing."

Buddy Hackett

#240

Maintain optimism and a sense of humor; enjoy the small pleasures in life.

So much of what you can accomplish depends on your attitude.

One of the best ways to maintain optimism is to have "a focus of hope." This means having goals that you strive toward with the hope of creating better conditions for you and for those around you.

This diagram depicts your focus— where you are now and the journey you will have to make to get where you want to be. Many of life's endeavors involve a journey. You probably won't reach your goal tomorrow. You'll reach it over a period of time by working through a series of objectives and activities. The point here is this: Have fun and remain optimistic in the pursuit of your goal. Enjoy the journey. Some people become so obsessed with trying to achieve that they forget to have fun along the way.

GOAL

THE JOURNEY

"The Journey is the Destination"

YOU

Have a sense of humor. Doesn't it feel good to have a good laugh with your family, friends, or co-workers? It's good for you physically too. When you laugh, your brain releases endorphins, internal chemicals that give you a feeling of well-being and help you deal with pain. Endorphins are also released through strenuous, aerobic exercise. (You've probably heard of the runner's high.)

So enjoy life. Have fun.

"The most important decision you make is to be in a good mood."

Voltaire

"You grow up the day you have your first real laugh at yourself."

Ethel Barrymore

A Reflection on Living Life in the Present

The Station
By Robert Hastings

Tucked away in our subconscious minds is an idyllic vision. We see ourselves on a long, long trip that almost spans the continent. We're traveling by passenger train, and out the windows we drink in the passing scene of cars on nearby highways, of children waving at a crossing, of cattle grazing on a distant hillside, of smoke pouring from a power plant, of row upon row of corn and wheat, of flatlands and valleys, of mountains and rolling hillsides, of city skylines and village halls, of biting winter and blazing summer and cavorting spring and docile fall.

But uppermost in our minds is the final destination. On a certain day at a certain hour we will pull into the station. There will be bands playing and flags waving. And once we get there, so many wonderful dreams will come true. So many wishes will be fulfilled and so many pieces of our lives finally will be neatly fitted together like a completed jigsaw puzzle. How restlessly we pace the aisles, damning the minutes for loitering … waiting, waiting, waiting for the station.

However, sooner or later we must realize there is no one station, no one place to arrive at once and for all. The true joy of life is the trip. The station is only a dream. It constantly outdistances us.

"When we reach the station, that will be it!" we cry. Translated it means, "When I'm 18, that will be it! When I buy a new 450 SL Mercedes-Benz, that will be it! When I put the last kid through college, that will be it! When I have paid off the mortgage, that will be it! When I win a promotion, that will be it! When I reach the age of retirement, that will be it! I shall live happily ever after!"

Unfortunately, once we get "it," then "it" disappears. The station somehow hides itself at the end of an endless track.

"Relish the moment" is a good motto … It isn't the burdens of today that drive men mad. Rather, it is regret over yesterday or fear of tomorrow. Regret and fear are twin thieves who would rob us of today.

So, stop pacing the aisles and counting the miles. Instead, climb more mountains, eat more ice cream, go barefoot oftener, swim more rivers, watch more sunsets, laugh more and cry less. Life must be lived as we go along. The station will come soon enough.

#241

Learn how to stay calm.

You already know that it's important to control your emotions. But when you feel stressful, you can easily do and say things that you regret later. Listen to your body. If your breathing grows rapid and you tense up, you are preparing to fight or flee. Think about how you want to act. Don't let someone or something control your emotions. That's reactive behavior. Instead use this formula to be proactive. It's based on the theory of rational emotive therapy, as defined by the behavioral psychologist Dr. Albert Ellis in his book *A Guide to Rational Living.*

> *"He who cannot smile should not keep shop."*
>
> Chinese Proverb

The next time you have a different point of view with your boss, a co-worker, or a family member, think about this term:

Complementarity

It was defined by Dr. Niels Bohr, the Nobel prize winning physicist. He defined it as follows: "A great truth is a statement whose opposite is also a great truth."

Maybe you're both right! Collaborate to reach agreement.

C limate — You determine the climate. Do you want to be stressful and out of control? If you have a choice, you will probably choose to remain calm.

A ctivating event — An activating agent is what the other person says or does that triggers your response. Instead of having a reactive trigger response, strive for a proactive one.

L isten and think — Really listen to what the other person is saying. Don't let that person's emotional words deter you from listening to the real message. If you know what the real message is, then you can think about a proper response.

M ake a response — Respond with a proactive statement. Be calm and in control rather than stressful and out of control.

> *"Real human freedom is the ability to pause between the events of our lives and choose how we will respond."*
>
> Rollo May

Learning to stay calm in difficult people situations requires remembering these three points:

1. **Assess the situation.** ————

> Think about how you should act before taking action.

2. **Accept the other person.** ————

> If you learn to accept the other person, you will save yourself a great deal of stress and you will likely be much more productive. You can't change other people. They must want to change on their own. If they choose not to change, then try a different action or response with them.

3. **Distance yourself from** ————
   difficult people.

> There are people who prefer to go through life being difficult. They can make you very stressful. Don't buy into their behavior. Don't spend time with them that you feel is unproductive.

How Do People Deal With Stress?

Here are the results of a study that asked people how they deal with stress. The top five ways are:

1. Talking to a friend or family member
   (personal support system) 58%

2. Listening to Music..49%

3. Reading..49%

4. Watching TV (Don't overdo this one.) 44%

5. Exercising (Try this one before watching TV.)........................36%

Source: D'Arcy Masius Benton and Bowles, Inc.
Fears and Fantasies of the American Consumer. May, 1986.

■ ■ ■

"Never wrestle with a pig because you both get dirty and only the pig likes it."

(old saying)

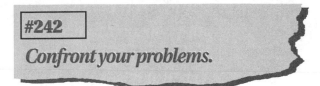

#242

Confront your problems.

Brooding about them only takes time away from high-payoff activities.

Meet your storms head on. Don't run away from them. Remember, the sun will come out again. Ethyl Kennedy, wife of the late Robert F. Kennedy, once said, "The birds still sing after the storm."

Bluebird Happiness

Bluebird, bluebird, I hear your song
Way up on top of the hill.

Why did you fly in such a haste
Away from my windowsill?

"I flew ahead of the storm," he said
With a peck and a hop and a trill.

"But the storm didn't come, you silly bird,
And I'll wager it never will."

"But the sky was black," came his muffled chirp,
"And the sun didn't show his face
And I couldn't sing without his smile
So I flew to another place."

"Bluebird, bluebird, you baffle me.
You're not living up to your form.
Happiness comes wherever you are
If you're not afraid of the storm."

Elizabeth M. Adams

CHAPTER 20

Focusing on the "P-Pod"

> *"We shall not cease from exploration, and the end of all of our exploring will be to arrive where we started and know the place for the first time."*
>
> T.S. Eliot

#243

Focus on the P-POD.

Productivity depends on:

Procrastination elimination

Organization

Discipline

So the P-POD is related to the idea that you can increase your productivity if you can take control of procrastination, overcome disorganization, and discipline yourself to follow through on your payoff priorities and goals.

The other topics in this book—such as controlling the telephone and interruptions, negotiating with your supervisor, and planning efficient meetings—are important and can help you to become more productive. However, if you can consistently concentrate on managing the three areas of the P-POD more effectively, you will take a giant step toward increasing your productivity and, thus, your success.

Reread the sections related to the POD (Procrastination, Chapter 14; Organization, Chapter 13; and Discipline, Chapter 9). Begin immediately to start new habits that will help you to overcome procrastination, get more organized, and be better disciplined. Be persistent and enjoy the results.

"Press on. Nothing in the world can take the place of persistence. Talent will not. Nothing is more common than unsuccessful men with talent. Genius will not. Unrewarded genius is almost a proverb. Education alone will not. The world is full of educated derelicts. Persistence and determination alone are omnipotent."

Calvin Coolidge

Enjoying Your Success

Two things we want as we strive to be more productive are results and success. Results are related to payoff: Are you working on the right things that produce the best results (highest payoff)?

Here again is the definition of success:

$$SUCCESS = \frac{DEFINED\ ACTIVITIES \times DIRECTED\ ACTION \times TIME\ ALLOCATED}{ANTICIPATED\ RESULTS\ (STANDARDS)}$$

This definition relates to the idea of moving toward the accomplishment of your important, high-payoff activities consistently—day after day.

Here are some final tips for achieving greater productivity and, thus, success:

#244 Share your knowledge.

Assist other people. Give them your expertise. Let others learn from you.

#245 Use recognition.

Reward other people for what they do well. Take time to let others know that you appreciate them. Recognize yourself for your own achievements.

#246 Challenge yourself and others.

Don't give up. Don't procrastinate or be a perfectionist. Always strive to complete your activities and projects and to do so within your deadlines.

#247 Create winners.

Give people the resources they need to accomplish their goals, activities, and projects. Create an atmosphere for people to excel.

#248 Enthuse yourself and others.

Approach life with vigor and excitement. Sure, you will have setbacks, but consistently maintain a demeanor of enthusiasm. It may rub off on others. Mickey Rooney said: "Enthusiasm is like manure. If it sits in a big pile it stinks. If you spread it around, something might grow."

#249 Stay close to people you work with.

Become their support system. Be their friend. Provide them with guidance and really listen to them when they are trying to provide you with information and direction. If you do, they will likely help you too. Be a bridge builder.

#250 Strive for quality work.

Accept nothing less. Sometimes people misinterpret productivity as doing more with less. Productivity is really doing the high-payoff activities consistently and with high quality. Consider this phrase: "Quality in everything we are and everything we do."

This book begins with these words: "This book on productivity will excite you about the possibilities and potential your life offers and motivate you to action."

You have read all the ideas for leading a fuller, happier, and more productive life. Pick and choose the ones you feel can best benefit you. Concentrate on achieving a balance—happiness at work and at home. When you go to bed each night, you should be able to reflect on the day and say to yourself: "I did something important today. I took action."

Finally consider the message of this poem by Nadine Stair, who was in her eighties when she wrote it.

Afterward: If I Could Live It Over ...

If I had to live my life over again
I'd dare to make more mistakes next time.
I'd relax.
I would limber up.
I would be sillier than I have been this trip.
I would take fewer things seriously.
I would take more chances.
I would take more trips. I would climb more mountains, swim more rivers.
I would eat more ice cream and less beans.
I would perhaps have more actual troubles, but I'd have fewer imaginary ones.
You see, I'm one of those people who lives seriously and sanely, hour after hour, day after day.
Oh, I've had my moments. And if I had it to do over again, I'd have more of them.
In fact, I'd try to have nothing else, just moments, one after another, instead of living so many years ahead of each day.
I've been one of those persons who never goes anywhere without a thermometer, a hot water bottle, a raincoat, and a parachute.
If I had it to do again, I would travel lighter than I have.
If I had to live my life over, I would start barefoot earlier in the Spring and stay that way later in the Fall.
I would go to more dances.
I would ride more merry-go-rounds.
I would pick more daisies.